Mini-Books are designed to
inform and entertain you.

They cover a wide range of
subjects—from Yoga to Cat-Care,
from Dieting to Dressmaking,
from Spelling to Antiques.

Mini-Books are neat
Mini-Books are cheap
Mini-Books are exciting

DISH GARDENS, JUNGLE JARS AND PUDDLE POTS

is just one Mini-Book
from a choice of many.

Recently published in Corgi Mini-Books

BEAUTY AND YOU
A CAREER FOR YOUR DAUGHTER
A CAREER FOR YOUR SON
COLLECTING CHEAP CHINA AND GLASS
THE DIET BOOK FOR DIET HATERS
DRESSMAKING—THE EASY WAY
FLOWER ARRANGEMENT
GIVING PARTIES
HAIR CARE
HOME NURSING AND FAMILY HEALTH
INDOOR PLANTS
JAMS, CHUTNEYS AND PRESERVES
LOOKING AFTER YOUR CAGED BIRD
THE MAGIC OF HONEY
MONTH BY MONTH IN YOUR KITCHEN
NAME YOUR DAUGHTER
NAME YOUR SON
NO TIME TO COOK BOOK
SHAPE UP TO BEAUTY
YOUR WEDDING GUIDE
THE YOUTH SECRET
SLIM THE FRENCH WAY

VIOLET STEVENSON

DISH GARDENS, JUNGLE JARS AND PUDDLE POTS

A MINI-BOOK BY CORGI

DISH GARDENS, JUNGLE JARS
AND PUDDLE POTS

A MINI-BOOK 552 76378 0

PRINTING HISTORY
Mini-Book Edition published 1971
Copyright © 1971 Violet Stevenson

Mini-Books are published by Transworld Publishers Ltd.,
Cavendish House,
57–59 Uxbridge Road, Ealing,
London, W.5
Filmset in Photon Times 12 pt. by
Richard Clay (The Chaucer Press), Ltd., Bungay, Suffolk
Printed in Great Britain by
Fletcher & Son Ltd., Norwich, Norfolk

CONTENTS

Chapter		Page
I	Gardens at your Fingertips	7
II	All about Plants you can Use	15
III	Types of Container	36
IV	Planting the Dish Garden	44
V	Jungle Jars	61
VI	Puddle Pots	83
VII	Nature's Prepacks	100
VIII	Rejuvenating, Replanting and Doctoring	117

CHAPTER I

GARDENS AT YOUR FINGERTIPS

Let me begin by saying what fun growing house plants can be. Not only do they make a home because they furnish it with a touch of greenfinger magic that brings even an empty room to life but they also provide us with an absorbing hobby, one that is, literally, at our fingertips. It is a hobby for anyone, old or young, rich or poor, busy or leisured.

Like so many other things, it's not what you do but the way that you do it! A plant doesn't necessarily have to be something growing alone in a flower pot with a saucer underneath. Plants are like people, they enjoy company. They don't have to stand alone indoors. They can be grouped in your home just as they are grouped in the garden.

Once you accept that you do not have to aim for one plant, one pot, you will realise that there are so many ways they can be both grown and displayed. Looking around my cottage as I write I see that I have plant communities growing in containers which vary from an oyster shell which holds a mixture of tiny succulents; a wide pedestal flower vase filled with an assortment of gorgeous coleus, some 18 inches high and raised from seed; a glazed dish with a mixture of cacti and succulents grouped under a piece of driftwood; an old vegetable tureen and a large wash basin with more and larger types; an enormous brandy balloon holding an assortment of bromeliads, attractive low-growing cryptanthus, members of the pineapple family; a carboy holding an assortment of beautifully coloured house plants, ivy, peperomia, *Begonia rex* and others; through to a cider jar in which I have sown mixed cacti seeds already germinating and a large, dried, plastic lined bracket fungus filled with mixed ferns. Quite a selection, yet only a few.

Dish gardens, jungle jars and puddle pots, what attractive pictures they conjure up and how much more fun their names sound than mere flower pots and saucers. From the little that I have already described you will see that they can range from miniatures (I know of one lady who makes these in outsize coat buttons) to adventurous plantings as large as you wish or your premises will accommodate. You can make them for your own pleasure or to give away as presents, for these are things you can give to anyone, even to those who have everything!

Gardens in miniature appeal so strongly to so many people. Children like both to make them and to receive them. Judging by the many letters I receive they are a boon to those unfortunate people who are housebound. One bed-ridden lady wrote and told me that all her plants are ranged on a large tea trolley which stands at right angles to her window. This can easily be wheeled over to her bedside when she feels able to attend to her little collection, all at bed level. I once knew a blind man who collected cacti, of all things! His joy at receiving a little dish garden was touching to see. Each day he delicately explored each contour of every one of his plants. He learned to recognise them and their condition and even felt the needs of the soil with his knowing fingertips.

Plants inside jungle jars have the fascination of fish in an aquarium. They too live in a secret world of their own and much of their magic and mystery lies in this secrecy. The marvellous thing is that it is so easy to grow plants this way. The plants like it. In their own little world they can create their personal micro-climate and the nice thing about this is that they then demand so little attention from you. They just settle down to a long and happy life.

The analogy between plants and fish in an aquarium is not so strange, for plants really are like pets in many ways. Some, as you would expect, are more endearing than others. Some are easy to care for and others are too exotic, too demanding for all but the wealthy with their special equipment, the painstaking and those with a great deal of time on their hands. But, and here's another nice thing, because life in a glass jar is so protected it is often possible to keep plants growing this way which otherwise would die in the warm, dry and perhaps smoky atmosphere of a normal living room.

Like our pets, plants make only few demands but these few must be recognised, catered for and obeyed. They need clean air, regular feeding and watering, grooming and even displaying. Some enjoy a little outing from time to time too. My bowls of cacti and succulents spend the summer outdoors and are brought back before the frosts threaten, renewed and ready cleansed for their winter in the home. It always surprises me to see just what extra growth they have made during their stay out in the open air.

Almost all other plants will enjoy being stood outdoors in a warm summer shower, but beware of leaving them there too long as a prey for the probing greenfly, hungry slugs and snails or to be buffeted and rocked on their roots by winds.

House plants are as varied as all other kinds of plants. They come as trees, bushes, climbers, trailers, creepers and are herbaceous, shrubby and succulent. Some are temperamental and others are easy to grow, and fortunately there are many of the easy ones. Naturally we should take care to select only those which will respond to our purpose, our situation and, perhaps, our skill.

It is not really possible to give hard and fast rules for cultivation, for so much depends on the person concerned, the plants, their situation and the conditions under which they are grown. But there are certain easy kinds, such as cacti and some succulents, sansevieria and bromeliads or room pines. All of these can be watered at certain regular intervals or in a simple manner. I recommend these to the beginner or to the heavy handed, who may have found, like so many, that they have lost more plants by drowning than from any other cause.

Then there are those obliging plants at the other extreme that are almost aquatic in their tastes, or so adaptable to a water existence that they may constantly stand in a puddle. These include the cyperus, the grass-like acorus and many of the aeroids, members of the arum family. These also present few problems except when they are to be mixed with others which like to be dryer at the roots.

Those we choose to grow inside jars ought to be really slow growers, otherwise they will soon be climbing like Jack up his beanstalk from their own world out of the jar's mouth and into ours.

Most of the plants I shall mention in this book you can buy ready-made, as it were. They have been raised from seed or cuttings by the nurseryman and we buy them in very small pots, usually three inches across. Larger plants in larger pots are, of course, available and it is also possible to obtain some plants in tiny pots, known as 'thumbs'. As you will appreciate, the smaller the root size the easier it is to insert the plants through the narrow aperture of a jungle jar, carboy or similar container. Again, tiny plants are immature plants, which means that they have a long life ahead of them before they grow too large for their home.

There are a few plants, mainly annuals, which you can grow right from the beginning from seed. Others can be propagated in other ways and I shall deal with all methods in a later chapter.

Some of the most rewarding of all plants to raise from the beginning until they flower are those which grow from bulbs. Here again you do not have to follow tradition and simply plant three or five bulbs in a traditional round bulb bowl. They can be displayed much more attractively than that. Tall bulbs like some tulips and daffodils often look much more elegant and imposing in a pedestal flower vase than in a squat bowl. I like to see them grouped around some beautifully simple plant such as a dracaena or towering above a glossy philodendron. With bulbs you can make the prettiest little dish gardens, mixing flowering bulbs and flowering and foliage plants together. They are especially beautiful if you plan colour schemes. You can use bulbs to give a new look to a jaded bowl of plants and it is well worth while in autumn to plant a few small bulbs among the plants in your dish gardens or puddle pots to bring a touch of colour in spring and so make sure that your established gardens will greet the year in a proper manner.

CHAPTER II

ALL ABOUT PLANTS YOU CAN USE

The most successful dish gardens and jungle jars are those in which plants of the same tastes are growing together. Knowing which these are is not easy if you are new to indoor gardening, but there are a few plants which are instantly recognisable even to the uninitiated. Take cacti for example.

These are unlike all other plants, for they have no stems or leaves. Instead, the plant is a fleshy or succulent body carrying within itself its own considerable supply of moisture. There is one exception, the group Pereskieae, but this need not concern us now.

Most cacti, except the type epiphyllum which is known as the leaf-flowering cacti and which can tolerate a little shade, need a tremendous amount of sunlight, and bowls holding these plants may therefore be stood in a position that might be unsuitable for many other plants.

Succulent plants are often mistaken for cacti when these are judged by appearance only. Usually when we are discussing succulents we think of just a few familiar plants such as stonecrops, houseleeks, the chunky sempervivums or of sedums. But any family of plants can produce a succulent member, it really depends upon its environment and so we can have succulent vines, pelargoniums, euphorbias, lilies, groundsel and daisies, most of which are usually grown as plant curiosities. Pot succulents are often a little more temperamental than cacti and are not quite such good subjects for mixing in bowls. However, you can make lovely gardens using these plants alone, either for indoors or if you select the hardy kinds for outdoors also. One reassuring thing is that it is usually only the most tolerant kinds that one finds on sale.

Cacti need watering about once a week from March to September, beginning with a little water only at first and then gradually increasing the supplies in April and May. During summer you should water the plants liberally and it does them good to stand them out in a summer shower. You can if you wish, and as I have said earlier, let them actually live outside in summer, keeping them in full sun and never under trees where drips from the leaves can harm them. One is usually recommended to plunge their pots in sand or to stand them in frames, but this is not practical for everyone and I have found that they can be stood outside on a window sill, doorstep, on a balcony or a patio wall, where, incidentally, they can look most striking and attractive. One needs only to ensure that they cannot get blown over and damaged and that they are not forgotten and thus remain unwatered for long periods during a summer drought.

Water once a month during the rest of the year, on the colder and shorter days, giving them just sufficient to prevent the soil from drying out completely.

You may find a bowl well filled with happily growing cacti a little difficult to water and in this case it is best to lower the whole bowl gently into a larger vessel containing water until the soil surface is under water. Hold it there until the air bubbles stop rising to the surface, then allow the surplus water to drain away. This way the whole of the soil is uniformly moist. But remember that this method of watering is for the summer only; it is too much for the plants during winter.

Like most desert plants cacti can take low temperatures but not frosts. Even so I think it is best to keep them in a warm room during winter and always where the light is strongest for most of the time, in other words in a south-facing window.

I really would not recommend that you mix cacti with other kinds of house plants in bowls and you will find that there are so many species of such diversity that this is not really necessary. You can make attractive mixtures of strangely contrasting shapes, sizes and textures using only cacti. However, there are some succulents which look well with them, and should you buy a box of mixed 'cacti' specially for a dish garden you are quite likely to find one kind mixed with the other.

Succulents are also used with other house plants. *Sedum sieboldii* is a great favourite. Its chunky leaves are beautifully variegated and they grow alternately on long stems which are terminated by flat heads of rosy flowers which bloom in late summer or autumn. On nurseries such as Rochford's where they plant mixed bowls for market this sedum is usually placed quite near the rim of the bowl because its stems will flow over the edge so prettily.

This is one of the succulents which dies down

to rest in the winter and so is best plunged, that is, pushed into or planted in the arrangement, pot and all. In this way it can be removed and replaced by some other plant during its resting period. Alternatively, it can be knocked from its pot and its roots wrapped in polythene. This way the plant will not take up so much room in the bowl but it will have to be repotted for its resting period if it is to be saved for another year.

Rochea, crassulas and echeverias are other succulents which mix well. Another plant which seems to get along in almost any kind of plant community is the tall, spiky leaved sansevieria, sometimes unkindly called mother-in-law's tongue. This is an obliging plant, good with cacti or leafy plants and tolerant of both sun and shade, cool conditions and heat. In a plant mixture it should be planted in the centre of the container in soil which is a little higher than the soil just inside the rim. This way its roots remain well drained, a condition they prefer.

Echeverias, which are succulents and there are several types, form very lovely leaf rosettes, often attractively covered with a bloom like that on grapes. These rosettes look well set at the focal point of an arrangement of plants, or so arranged that they nestle at the foot of some attractive piece of rock, driftwood or bark. I have one particularly lovely dish garden which holds nothing else but one species of echeverias. It is a long and shallow oval bowl about 2 inches deep which originally held five rosettes and over the years these have produced offsets. Furthermore, any leaf which I accidentally knocked off when moving the dish and which was immediately pressed into any empty area within, has also grown into a plant so that now the dish is one great dense mass of lovely glaucous rosettes, like a bowl of thick, grey roses!

Other rosette plants are the bromeliads, which I have already mentioned a few times. These vary considerably from the small types of cryptanthus, sometimes called starfish plants and earth stars, to the large nidulariums and aechmeas. Both of these are unusual in shape and handsomely coloured, but they are not really so useful for little gardens as are the cryptanthus.

These bromeliads are among the easiest of all plants to grow, mainly because their watering is so uncomplicated. In their natural state most of them are epiphytes, growing on jungle trees, and they draw their sustenance from the air. The moisture in the humid air trickles down their leaves, cupped at their bases like a handy funnel, and collects in the centre of the plant. You will find the strange and dramatic flowers growing up through this tiny pool. In the home the best way to keep these plants watered is simply to make sure that this central reservoir is always kept filled. You can do this by pouring in water or using an atomiser or spray. Some of the water will escape through the leaf separations and reach the soil, but it is not necessary otherwise to water the soil at all. Indeed, if the soil is allowed to get too wet for too long the roots will rot. But an occasional dose of fertiliser can safely be applied this way.

Incidentally, you may be interested in making a bromeliad branch. It is possible to fix a community of bromeliads on to a branch or a piece of driftwood and let the plants grow and increase there. If you keep them well sprayed they will thrive. The branch, which should be attractively shaped, must be well anchored to take the weight of the plants, so choose a suitable base such as a low bowl or a plant trough. You can anchor the branch best by nailing its base to a foot made of two crossed pieces of wood. Measure this so that it fits snugly inside the container. Finally cover it with stones so that it is not only well hidden but held down securely.

The plants can be left in their pots or can have their roots wrapped in black polythene, and they can then be tied or wired to the branch. One or two more nestled in the stones below link the base with the branch. A bromeliad branch is a happy decoration for a garden room. The plants should be sprayed daily with clean, tepid water, rain water if possible.

Although in every case we should be sure to collect the correct plants for our purpose, the choice of plants which can be used for little indoor gardens is really wide. There are sufficient to allow us to mix them attractively and with reason, just as one does when mixing cut flowers in an arrangement. I think that one should try to provide contrast in shape, texture and habit. For instance, when you plant a tall, pointed subject such as a sansevieria, find a broad leaved shorter plant, such as *Peperomia magnoliaefolia* to complement it and place this near by.

Good broad-leaved plants are both plentiful and attractive. The handsome and beautifully coloured *Begonia rex*, for example, gets along well with other plants. There are many varieties of rex, all differently marked. The one drawback to this plant is that it does not like a dry atmosphere and tends to sulk in winter when the air in a home is hot and dry and even smoky, but planted in a carboy or some similar enclosed container it will thrive and remain lovely the year through.

Also beautifully marked are both the calatheas and marantas, nearly related and requiring much the same treatment. The chunky *Peperomia magnoliaefolia* already mentioned is another good tempered and attractively variegated plant for mixed bowls. There are other peperomias, all worth growing, including trailing kinds.

Most miniature gardens look their prettiest when a little plant or two is scrambling or trailing over the edge of the container. The popular and well known tradescantia is ideal for this purpose, especially if, when it has grown sufficiently, tips are kept pinched out so that it does not become too straggly and untidy as it is apt to do as it ages. (Don't forget you can root these tips, see Chapter VI.) The nearly related *Zebrina pendula* is extremely handsome, with a metallic sheen in the stripes on the upper sides of the leaves and rich purple undersides.

And what would we do without the hedera or

ivy? This plant is most varied, in both size and markings. The smallest leaved varieties grow slowly and so are particularly useful for our purpose. I love the thumbnail-sized leaves of Little Diamond, its newest leaves almost pure white.

Aspect is quite important for plants and although only a few can tolerate the glaring sun shining through glass most need good light, so you need to take into account the place where you intend to stand your bowls and jungle jars. As a general rule the more variegated the leaf the more light it needs and even here one must still guard against sun glare. The beautifully marbled *Scindapsus aureus* for example, will develop ugly brown spots on its leaves if it becomes burned.

For those whose homes are not sunlit or who haven't large windows there are still plenty of plants. There are many which love the gloom, for after all the jungle, whence so many of them came, is a gloomy place. Such plants will grow well back in a room away from the windows, in a dark hallway, on a staircase and in a north-facing room, so long as this is not too cold. The spathiphyllum, which produces elegant, arum-like flowers; *Syngonium podophyllum*; *Scindapsus aureus*, with yellow and bright green leaves (an exception to the rule that the variegated leaves must have good light) are a few you can grow. Many ferns like the shade and so do some of the darker-leaved ivies, although when these have been raised in a sunny greenhouse they sometimes drop a few leaves at the beginning until they have become acclimatised.

One of my great favourites is *Plectranthus oertendahlii*, which is too seldom seen on sale. Such an easy and adaptable plant should be more widely grown. Fortunately cuttings root easily in water alone. I like to use it on the edge of one of my ladder-type bookshelves from which it cascades down delightfully, turning its leaves, hairy, greenish-purple, to face the window on the other side of the room.

So far I have not mentioned the lovely flowering plants, of which there are so many, which can be grown also in bowl gardens. In most cases, however, these need to be treated as temporaries rather than permanent tenants like the foliage plants, for they are generally at their best only when they are actually in flower. But so long as they harmonise and look well with the plants already growing in the bowl there really is no limit to the kind of plant you use.

If you like flowering plants and prefer to use

more than one in any bowl garden you make then it is as well to make provision for it when you are filling the bowl. You can do this by 'planting' one or more empty flower pots. When you are ready to install the flowering plant all you need to do is to remove the empty pot and drop in the flowering replacement. And in extension of the same practice, when one flowering plant has passed its best it can easily be removed and replaced with one which is just approaching its peak.

Some, but only few, flowering plants also have fine foliage and of these possibly the cyclamen is best known. Some modern varieties of *C. decora* have handsome marbled leaves, so lovely that it is worth growing the plant for these alone. But of course there are flowers also, a long succession of them if you grow the plant well.

Remember that it is best to buy or to use flowering plants which are not yet at their best. Not only do those in bud transplant better but you can enjoy them for a longer period. If you go to buy a plant which is in bloom, first take a careful look at it to see if there are more buds to come. And while on the same subject, never buy greenhouse plants which are on display out of doors in winter, for they are sure to have suffered from their change in atmosphere, even if the day is not frosty.

Generally speaking it is best to choose small and low-growing flowering plants, otherwise you may find that these dominate the others. Furthermore, little plants are usually cheapest, easier to raise yourself and certainly less trouble to replace than the larger specimens.

The range seems to grow each year. Little azaleas are often used effectively at the focal point of a gift arrangement by nurserymen who make bowl gardens and you also will find these adaptable and obliging plants. They stand transplanting well, but you must take care always to see that the fibrous root ball does not become dry. The more bloom that appears on the plant the more water the azalea will require. Try to let it stay in its own pot if possible. Primulas of all kinds, including the less exotic primroses, both the common yellow species and the coloured varieties, look very attractive with glossy green plants. (On occasion I have cheated and placed a posy of primroses and their leaves in a little container of water instead of a flowering plant. I also do this with posies of snowdrops and other early spring flowers.)

Saintpaulias or African violets are extremely popular and so long as you do not expect them to last for many months these can also be mixed with other plants. Actually these also look quite lovely when grown together, several plants in a large container, and in this case they seem to have a much longer life. Being perennial, they flower again and again. They dislike polluted air, even too much tobacco smoke will upset them sometimes, and because of this they too are plants which benefit from being grown inside glass, in a fish tank or a glass battery jar for example. Sometimes one sees a saintpaulia growing inside a goldfish bowl. The plants may either be transplanted into good potting compost or merely plunged, their pot rims being placed just below the surrounding peat.

The succulent crassulas, rochea and sometimes the berry-bearing shrubs such as solanums, are all suitable and will add a little colour or seasonal interest to a dish garden.

Heathers also add colour and are always available in the shops in winter, but in my opinion they do not always harmonise well with the majority of house plants, perhaps because their foliage is so fine and they are of such indeterminate shape. I do not like them with any of the large, glossy-leaved plants. However, they do look quite well with small leaved ivies, tradescantia, chlorophytum and cyperus.

Each year I like to grow and use small plants of coleus, a foliage plant sometimes called ornamental nettle because of the shape of its leaves and not because it can sting. The seedlings are easily raised on a warm window sill. When these are large enough to handle, instead of pricking them out each into individual pots, I fill bowls and large flower vases with a dozen or more, all assorted and very gay. They soon make a fine decoration and the plants will go on growing for months so long as they are well watered and fed regularly. I find also that a coleus is as bright and useful as a flowering plant for giving a new look to an old dish garden. It should be removed when it becomes too large. Also, and this goes for all of them, the spiky flowers should be nipped out of the tips of the stems as soon as they appear, as this helps to keep the plants compact, vigorous and leafy.

It is possible to lift some plants from the garden and use these quite successfully, and these are especially welcome in early spring when they will respond to the gentle forcing they get from the warmth of the average home and bloom earlier than they would have done out of doors. I have used the wild celandines this way as well as primroses, daisies and various alpines in pots. All live for quite a long time and all can be replanted in the garden, or in the wild, when they are finally removed from the dish.

Small bulb flowers of the kinds that grow in clumps, such as crocuses, snowdrops and scillas, also look lovely. Lift them when the flower buds are just ready to open. This is often a much better way of displaying them than trying to raise these particular plants in pots, because they do not force well. Autumn crocuses and colchicum are very beautiful and so easy to grow. They will even bloom out of soil. (See Chapter on Bulb Flowers.) Their colours look so well with all the house plants and they are unexpected in the autumn and therefore doubly welcome.

A word about colour harmonies. You will find that even in a so-called green plant there is more than one colour or hue. Quite often the stems, veins, bracts, stipules or undersides carry vivid colours, although sometimes these may be only in small quantities. However, it is worth studying these tiny areas of colour when you plan what plants to bring together, for it is surprising how much more effective and beautiful a dish garden with a considered colour scheme can be.

In fact, one finds that a floral colour can enhance and emphasise the foliage hues in such a way that one is surprised to see just how colourful is the leaf. So many of the yellow, cream and white variegated plants look lovely with spring bulb flowers such as narcissi, including daffodils, yellow hyacinths and short golden or white tulips. Those plants with that special vivid red in their leaves are so easy to match with many pretty flowering plants, from the humble busy lizzie, impatiens, to the flamboyant anthuriums and the graceful cyclamen. There are others that are touched with amethyst and rose hues. There is never any difficulty in finding plants to go with these.

There is a different kind of dish garden, one that uses no house plants and one that you can create at very little cost. Yet it is one which, I am sure, will bring you a great deal of pleasure and interest. This is a miniature forest. Each autumn there are millions of seeds all around us, dropped from our native trees. Many of these are worth collecting and sowing. So when you go for your winter walks keep a good look out for acorns, beechnuts, conkers, ash keys, hornbeam, maple and the rest, including berries. Collect some leafmould if you will not be acting illegally. Alternatively use potting compost or garden soil.

Plan your forest before you begin sowing the seeds. You can make hills and valleys by heaping the soil, supporting it by stones in the manner described in the next chapter. Look out also for some attractive stones on your walks; you may find a mossy stone or two lying on a bank or the edge of a stream.

Use a fairly shallow dish as a container. After you have planned it and sown the seeds where they are to grow, finish off the surface by strewing sand or laying moss on it. Now, as the seeds or berries have not yet been stratified, you should let your little forest stand outdoors to let it become frozen once or twice. After this you can bring it indoors and stand it in a sunny window. Be sure to keep the soil moist but not sodden. Incidentally, you will find that some seeds will germinate much faster than others.

Not all of the seedlings will go on growing for years. Certainly not if you keep the forest indoors all the time, but they might if you can find a place for them in the open. I grow mine on a shelf on the sheltered side of a carport which is open to the air but protected from the worst of the weather. It really depends on how good or how green are the fingers that look after them. But even so, while they are growing for a year or two at least they will bring you a great deal of fun and entertainment.

If you would prefer to grow individual trees to plant out later, remember that most of them, and certainly the berries such as holly and hawthorn, will need to be stratified before they will germinate properly. To do this take a flower pot one-third full of sand, pour a layer of seeds or berries on to this and top up the pot with at least an inch or so of more sand. Plunge the pot up to its rim in the ground if you have a garden, or stand it on your balcony or window-sill if you haven't. Cover it with wire netting against field mice if you live in the country. Let the pot remain in the ground all winter so that the seeds become frosted and then sow them in the spring.

Besides the wild seeds there are others from which you can grow similar plants and make similar bowl or dish gardens. These include lemons, oranges, grapefruits and other fruit pips. These will not need to be stratified for they come from warmer countries. On the contrary, they are more likely to need heat, and one of the best ways to get them to germinate is to start them off in the airing cupboard unless you are fortunate enough to have a greenhouse or a propagating case.

As we progress through this little book I shall introduce you to more plants suitable for bowls or dishes, but for the moment let us consider those which are particularly suitable for bottle gardens and jungle jars. As I said earlier, slow growing plants are essential, otherwise you will run into problems. It is also best to select those which have flexible leaves which will not become damaged as the plants are dropped or squeezed into the jars as some have to be. There are many, as I said, which cannot stand the open atmosphere of a home where there is no great humidity, as there is in the jungle proper or in a well-run greenhouse, but which thrive in the micro-climate of a closed or almost enclosed jar. Among these perhaps the most gorgeous is the codiaeum or croton. Other lovely leaves grow on calathea, fittonia, the small leaved variegated fig *Ficus radicans*, maranta, peperomia, pellaea, pilea, pellionia and the cryptanthus I have already mentioned.

For contrasts of shape there are the upright

cyperus, really a waterside plant and another aquatic, the variegated sedge carex, with its attractive umbels. Tiny palms such as cocos, phoenix and neanthe give elegance and have an exotic air.

As ground covers there are several species of a moss- or fern-like plant selaginella, all very dainty, and another little mat-like plant *Nertera depressa* which bears bright orange berries gleaming like strange pearls.

If you like ferns you can make a delightful collection of these, but make sure that they are the true ferns, which *Asparagus plumosus* and *A. sprengeri* are not. These grow much too large.

CHAPTER III

TYPES OF CONTAINER

At one time it was said that it was impossible to use glazed containers without drainage holes as plant containers and that plants grown in them would surely die. But this has not proved to be the case. There is really no limit to the type of container which can be used, although none must be so shallow that they will not hold sufficient of the essential water. Even so, certain fairly shallow containers, a large old-fashioned meat dish for example, can be used very effectively if the soil is raised in places and little plateaux made for some plants with the aid of rocks, pieces of cork bark or driftwood. So long as a container is waterproof, or can be made so in order that it will not damage furniture or anything else on which it stands, it will do for a dish garden. Jungle jars are discussed a little further on.

Obviously it is best to search for something

which suits its surroundings, that fits in with its environment as well as something which suits the plants. Dish gardens in my garden room, which has rough stone and wooden walls, need quite different containers from those in, say, my bedroom.

For those who live in modern surroundings there are many beautiful and distinctive pieces of modern ceramic, metal, glass, wood and even plastic which can look absolutely splendid filled with plants, and it is an odd fact that although they must be as ancient as the hills, many house plants have an intriguing contemporary look about them.

On the other hand there is no lack of antique containers, even period pieces, for those who do not like to mix one style with another. And here again one finds that there are plants, or rather mixtures of plants, that have about them an Edwardian, Victorian or even earlier charm. Mixing plants really is not very different from arranging the flowers, and it is usually the container which sets the style.

Unusual containers give character to a dish garden and help it blend with its surroundings. My own range from a large copper preserving pan, a Georgian foot bath, a wine cooler, copper coal scuttle, wash basins, bird baths, lidless tureens of all shapes and sizes, vases, troughs and dishes bought originally for flower arrangement, to shells of many sizes and kinds.

I take the precaution of lining all metal containers with polythene. Often one can find a bag which is of a suitable size, a garbage bin liner for example. One bag inside another to make two thicknesses makes doubly sure. I do not think that the metal would affect the plants, but certainly the soil affects metals and can stain it badly. Lined with plastic there is no trouble so long as one takes care when watering that no moisture trickles down between the plastic and the metal.

The warm texture and colour of copper suits the glossy green of so many plants and the metal itself is distinctive enough to carry plants which themselves are highly individual. And I like pewter tones and textures harmonising with the metallic finish of some begonia leaves and also with the pretty amethyst and the metallic sheen present in the leaves of tradescantia and zebrina. Brass, as one would expect, suits the yellow-leaved plants and together, coloured plants and shining brass, they bring a delightful sunshine effect to a room.

Incidentally, a good and safe way of cleaning the metal containers when they are full is to draw a polythene bag over the plants. Tuck its edge down inside the rim of the container and then polish away. This way the leaves do not come in contact with the metal polish, neither do they become accidentally bruised or damaged as you work.

If you are thinking of making dish gardens as gifts, a browse around junk stalls will prove invaluable. Besides little containers of all kinds you will find many vessels which have lost their lids but can still be used for this purpose. Alternatively, many objects about the house or stored away in the attic may suit your plants surprisingly well. Baskets, wickerwork and all wooden objects have a natural affinity with plants and these can be lined with strong polythene to make them waterproof. Apart from old fruit baskets given a coat of paint, work baskets, garden trugs and log baskets, I have seen old wooden cutlery boxes, tea caddies, cradles and other pieces of treen used most effectively and looking so much at home in their new role. Kitchenware is another good source of supply: brightly coloured saucepans and casseroles which have lost some of their enamel, jelly moulds, deep meat dishes and ovenware of all kinds, even a pair of scales can be used.

One of the prettiest fern gardens I have made was in an outsize fungus I found growing in a hollow lime tree and later dried in the airing cupboard. And I have also a large, spoon-shaped piece of driftwood which is a great favourite, especially for cryptanthus and other bromeliads. Both of these have to be lined to render them watertight. A large marble mortar holds an assortment of succulents.

Teapots, cups and saucers, fruit dishes and shells are just a few more which can be used mainly as puddle pots, where plants are grown entirely in water or water and pebbles.

If you have a choice it is worth bearing in mind that a container with sides that slope so that the mouth of the vessel is much wider than the base gives you plenty of soil surface on which the plants can display themselves. If the container is deep, four inches at least, there is room for some roots near the base to go down to the bottom and for others to be spread out nearer the surface.

As these containers have no drainage hole such as that which provides an outlet for water in the conventional flower pot, one must instead install a layer of drainage material at the base of the container beneath the soil. This provides air spaces into which the water will be rapidly sucked when the plants are watered. This rapid downward flow (at least, it should be rapid, and this is one reason why one should allow the soil to become almost dry before re-watering) brings air with it. This air in turn provides oxygen to the roots and helps to aerate the soil and keep it sweet. Many plants die from drowning. So much water is given to them that there is never space left in the soil for air and the roots sicken, rot and die.

Most people make a drainage layer by spreading crocks (small pieces of broken earthenware flower pot), small stones or shingle or even washed clinker on the base of the container. On this is sometimes spread a few nuggets of charcoal to keep sweet any water which might lie in the bottom of the container. The charcoal absorbs the harmful gases which stagnant water gives off. However, I have found that it is best to use charcoal entirely for this drainage layer. Not many of us can easily find crocks in these days when the earthenware pot is becoming more and more replaced by plastic. Stones and shingle tend to make a bowl very heavy. Charcoal can be bought from chemists and hardware stores. It is inexpensive, light in weight yet bulky, and should you wish can be used again and again. How the gardens are planted and what soils should be used are discussed in the next chapter.

So far as jungle jars are concerned, once again there appears to be no limit to the type of container unless it is one of supply and demand. The large glass carboys, once so common, like the earthenware flower pots, are being replaced by plastic. I imagine they will soon become collectors' pieces. However, there are many more suitable glass vessels, from goldfish bowls, battery jars, old fashioned sweet and modern storage jars, outsize brandy balloons to Victorian glass domes. I have also an old London copper street lamp which makes a most unusual and attractive jungle jar.

As one who has spent a lot of time making flower arrangements I have, as you would expect, many tall or pedestal flower vases. Quite a number of these are used for displaying house plants. My objection to flat bottomed dishes, troughs and bowls is that they tend to limit both the way plants can be arranged and the way in which they grow. When, for instance, you use a vase with a pedestal foot, the plants are lifted well above the level of the table on which the container is to stand. This gives elegance to the arrangement. It means also that any plant which tends to trail or lean over the rim of the container can be encouraged to do so even further. When you have to move the garden you can do so by holding a portion of the pedestal well away from the plants and so you will be unlikely to damage any of those which trail. These will also not be damaged as they might be if they were trailing on the table itself.

CHAPTER IV

PLANTING THE DISH GARDEN

When you are ready to plant your dish garden, or any other indoor garden for that matter, do not make the mistake of going into the garden or the countryside to dig up a bucket of soil. If you do you are almost certainly going to bring indoors many things other than the necessary soil! In it are likely to be millions of weed seeds, fungi spores and insect pests. And quite likely also, the particular sample of soil you have collected will either be too limy, too acid, too dense or too porous for your purpose, and if you use it your plants may never thrive.

Today it is possible to buy a selection of blended soils or composts, as they are often called, which are not only sterile (which means that they contain no live seeds, spores or pests) but which are also correctly balanced to support plants in the manner to which they have been accustomed.

You can get seed sowing composts as well as potting composts. You can also buy mixtures specially for cacti, although these plants will almost always grow quite well in one of the general mixtures. Some even do surprisingly well in the peaty Levington compost.

Not all of these composts are based on soil, but the original, the famous John Innes composts are. Their name comes from the fact that it was at the John Innes Horticultural Institution that the recipes for these composts were evolved after much experiment and investigation. So the J.I. composts, as they are generally known, are not proprietary products, but those which have been strictly prepared according to the formulas laid down and published by the Institution.

Unfortunately samples sometimes vary, and occasionally a nurseryman will tell you that he makes his own J.I. compost without using sterilised soils. All true J.I. composts must consist of sterilised soils and other ingredients in the correct proportions, so go always to a reputable supplier or for a well-known branded name. Many chain stores sell J.I. composts in small quantities in labelled bags. Prices will vary only by a few pence according to the different producers.

If you do not have to count the cost of time and labour, obviously it is cheaper to mix your own compost, and if you wish to do this you will find the recipes at the end of this chapter, but of course it is much easier to buy them ready mixed.

I use a small soil sterilising unit which holds a bushel of soil and which cost about £5 some years ago. It plugs into an electric point on the garage wall and is really very little trouble to use. The greatest expenditure of time and labour goes in the careful and accurate blending of the various ingredients.

Incidentally, it is not wise to buy or make very much more than you need at one time, even though it may seem much more economical to buy a large bag or mix a quantity. This is because the soil mixture deteriorates during storage and there is always the risk of wind blown seeds or fungal spores drifting into the mixture.

But soil is heavy and for someone who lives above ground level and has no lift, the transport of a large bag of soil mixture can offer real problems. However, there are now certain soil-less composts which are based instead on specially processed peat, very much lighter in weight. These are also marketed in small quantities in carry-home bags by some chain stores and all garden shops.

All these composts have the requisite plant foods and mineral salts included in the mixture. This means that any plant grown in them should normally be provided for and nourished for the first six months or so. One has to consider that plant foods from soils and composts in pots both becomes used up by the plants and leached out when the plants are watered. The loss is nothing like so great when containers have no drainage holes, which is one reason why a drainage layer is so necessary, for otherwise the build-up of plant foods could sometimes be damaging.

After about six months one should begin giving plants some supplementary form of plant food or fertiliser. It is best to use a liquid or soluble plant food and to apply this as and when the plants are watered at regular intervals. There are many good plant fertilisers marketed. Follow directions carefully and remember if you are of a generous nature that plants can be killed by too much feeding.

So the first rule for a successful dish garden is to provide good soil from the beginning.

Before I explain how to plant a dish I should

point out that when plants are moved you should always make sure they are re-planted at the same level in the soil. The depth is determined by their crowns, the part of the plant at the junction of roots and top. The crown should never be further above or below the new soil level than it was originally and you will be able to see the mark on the stem. Keep to this level.

Thus you will see that there is a maximum and minimum depth of soil according to the plants you are going to use. You will need to watch carefully when plants from varied sizes of pots are to be planted together. Bear in mind that in the finished arrangement the soil surface does not have to be level. It can be raised in the centre, to the side, or in the case of some gardens, a Japanese garden or a 'forest' for example, you can make one or more 'hills' and plateaux if the garden is large enough and the plants are suitable.

Making raised soil areas not only gives a plant a greater depth for its roots, but also raises it and lends it height. This is sometimes essential when plants are roughly of the same size and habit.

It is also advisable to select these higher situations for such plants as like to be well drained and comparatively dry at the roots, sansevierias, chunky leaved peperomias and most succulents are examples.

If you intend to use stones to make a simple rock garden effect, be sure to have the stones ready when you begin assembling the garden. There is no objection to using mossy stones from the hedgerow if you like these. I often use them myself. But in this case you will be wise to inspect the stones just to make sure that no woodlice, earwigs, slugs or other predators likely to feed on your plants are lurking in the crevices. If you soak the rocks in warm water (not hot or you will kill the moss) for a few minutes you will encourage any insect tenant to leave its home.

I find that small, chunky, attractively shaped pieces of driftwood are as much use and certainly as attractive as stones. These can be used to support the soil when plateaux are to be made, and they can also be used to tilt plants, to isolate one from another, to hide the rim of the flower pot, or even to hide, support or wedge a pot which has to be stood on the surface of the soil rather than plunged into it. Alternatively pieces of cork bark can be used.

Taller pieces of driftwood make attractive supports for climbing plants and they help to give height and interest generally to a plant arrangement. An advantage of driftwood is that it is free from insect pests, apart from the fact that its sun, sea and sand polished textures and sculpted shapes are so beautiful. You must make sure, though, that it is securely anchored before you begin planting.

While on the subject of using wood, I can perhaps point out that many bromeliads can be induced to grow in the wood itself, somewhat in the manner in which they would grow on trees in their native state as I described earlier. You need not make an entire bromeliad branch, but you often can decorate a branch with one or two small plants.

Sphagnum moss tied around the roots of plants, first knocked from their pots, keeps them both moist and nurtured. This way the roots are well protected from the harsh, dry air. In time the plant's roots will grow directly into the wood.

Pieces of coral and the aquarium rocks, often raw glass, sold in pet shops are also attractive, especially if the plants have some of the same colours in their leaves, veins or stems. I also use sea shells. Large examples look well displayed among plants, even with a trailer planted in them.

Smaller shells are useful to spread over the soil surface to cut down the rate of evaporation. It really depends on how much landscaping you intend to carry out. The shells have a natural affinity with the plants and some of the rough textured oysters, for example, make fine 'rocks' and are so easy to use.

Sea fans, also obtainable from the pet stores, are both useful and attractive for placing at the back of a bowl or dish to support a frail climber or even merely to act as an unusual backcloth. I use flat scallop shells in the same way in tiny gardens and I also use these same shells as a base, one to hold a smaller shell in which I plant tiny succulents. I fix one to the other with plaster before the planting begins.

All accessories will need securing firmly. Although some items can merely be placed on the soil surface, more generally some portion will need to be anchored well below soil level. A good way of holding a lightweight branch is to use an upturned flower pot and to insert the end of the branch through the drainage hole. The flower pot can then be covered with sand.

Children love to make 'Japanese' gardens and it is usually possible to buy packets of little figures to decorate and inhabit the gardens. These are often made attached to a spike or pin which you can push into the soil to hold the pieces in place.

When you assemble any garden you need to have some idea of how you are going to site the ornaments (if you intend to use any) before you begin planting. So far as Japanese gardens are concerned. I find that the temple or pagoda looks best situated on a rise in the ground and should have a 'tree' growing at its side. You need a path up to the temple and this is where tiny shells or coarse sand are useful. Flat pieces of gravel can be used as paving slabs.

Children like to have a 'pool' in such gardens and a little handbag mirror can be used for this. It is so easy to make its edges less formal and rectangular by placing flat stones, shells and overhanging plants around the margins of the 'water'.

Pebbles gathered from the seashore can be used in all types of gardens and one can make landscapes less coy than those of a Hong Kong type Japanese garden. The lovely shapes, colours and textures of some pebbles look so well with plants chosen to harmonise with them. Soak the pebbles first to remove all traces of salt.

Before you begin planting have all your acces-

A JAPANESE BOWL GARDEN

Made in a deep plate and filled with cacti, succulents and one 'tall' dwarf conifer. This will need replacing for it will not live as long as the others indoors. Alternatively, a 'tree'-like succulent could be used in its place. To the left of this is one of the so-called prickly pear cacti, opuntia. To its right is a cereus and to the right of this column-like cactus are two types of crassula, both succulents. The globular cactus is an echinopsis. In the foreground, left, is a grey-green echeveria, a succulent. To the right of the bridge is another, an aloe this time, and far right is an astrophytum, a cactus.

The surface is sand with tiny stones, sold for this purpose, scattered on it to give areas of both green and orange to match the ornaments.

sories ready and make sure that you have properly devised ways of using and securing them.

Having selected what plants you intend to grow together it is a good plan to arrange them on the table before planting in roughly the pattern you intend to create. You will then be able to see what placement is really practical and where the tallest or shortest plant ought to go.

Always water the plants and let them drain well before you knock them from their pots. Never use a plant with roots so dry that the soil is dust. In this case, water and wait a while. It is best to knock them out from their pots as you proceed. This can be done quite easily and quickly without damaging either plant or pot.

Take the pot in one hand and slide the first two fingers of the other hand on each side of the main stem or the crown of the plant, well below any leaves, the hand resting on the pot rim. Turn the pot upside down and with the plant itself held well away from the edge (which might damage the leaves) give the rim of the pot a sharp tap on the side of the table. The soil or root ball should then come away quite cleanly, rather like a sandpie leaves its pail. All you have to do is to turn the plant the right way up again.

You will very likely find that, knocked from its pot, the ball of soil is too deep for the new container in which it is to go. But it is possible to rearrange this pot-shaped mass without injuring the roots. One must take great care though, for as I warned earlier the less the roots are disturbed the more readily will the plant settle down in its new home.

Often one finds that if the drainage crock or little piece of perforated metal which may be adhering to the base of the roots is carefully removed, one can then shake away a great deal of loose soil, thus making it easier to spread the roots out, umbrella-like, should this be necessary, taking great care not to break the fibrous roots.

Arrange the plant roots on the soil. Determine whether and where the soil needs raising, and holding each plant so that it stands upright (or at some other angle should you desire it, for plants intended to trail over the edge are sometimes better if they are slightly tilted) cover the roots with soil. Press this down firmly so that the plant is as solidly anchored as if it had been growing this way always, but do not make the soil surface so hard that water cannot penetrate it. Soil must always be aerated.

When all the plants are in position water them carefully, preferably by spraying the leaves and the soil surface so that both are well moistened but not sodden. Stand the dish where it will not receive the full sun for the first few days.

Many cacti are very prickly, so handle them with care. Pick up the plants with a thick but soft cloth or wear strong gloves, perhaps even both. Some spines (glochids) are poisonous and should be extracted from the skin immediately should you become pricked by them. Others, like those of the opuntia, merely irritate. If a spine is so embedded or so tiny as to be invisible, a good tip is to apply a piece of transparent adhesive tape to the spot. Let it remain there for a minute or two and then peel it off. Usually the spine will come away with it.

When you have finished filling the bowl the soil level should be at least half an inch below the rim to allow for easy watering. The best way to water apart from immersion is to pour enough in to fill this area between the soil surface and the rim of the container. If the soil is in the correct condition and the drainage is right, the water should soon disappear beneath the soil surface.

Perhaps here it would be as well to give a few

hints about watering. As I said earlier, it is quite impossible for me to tell you how often the average leafy house plant will need water. It is possible to give rough rules for cacti, as I have, but watering all others will depend on how warm, dry and sunny is the room in which they are living. In my own home all the plants are looked at carefully once a week, but sometimes, especially in sunny weather, one will see some plants wilting or flagging.

As you might expect, I can tell by looking at a plant whether or not it is thirsty, but this is not so easy for a new gardener. One good way is to lift the bowl or pot and judge by the weight. Another method is gently but sharply to tap the bowl on the assumption that if it is dry it will ring with a clearer, more ringing note than if the soil is wet.

If you make a practice of spraying the foliage of the plants with clear, tepid water you will have to take this into account when judging whether or not the plants need water at the roots. Take care when spraying that the root soil does not become sodden. It is even advisable under some circumstances to cover or protect the soil during spraying with a piece of plastic sheeting or newspaper. I would say that when in doubt it is nearly always safest to let the plants go a little longer without water than to give them some just in case. Remember that water can easily and quickly be applied, but that an excess of water can take many days to dry out, causing possible damage to the plant during the whole of this time.

I have more than once returned home after a few days away to find certain plants bowed over their containers because they were limp from want of water. Quick first aid, usually by immersing the bowl or pot just under the surface of a bucket or sink of water, has had a most dramatic effect and in no time at all (or so it seems) one watches the plants being restored to their former healthy and turgid state. I quote this not as an example to follow, but as a suggestion that often a short spell of drought does little real harm. One can always console oneself with the knowledge that, anyway, the dry soil is bound to have been wonderfully aerated!

Earlier on I suggested that one should transplant crowns of plants back to their original level and there is another point about crowns to observe. This is that some plants do not like to have water poured over their crowns; cyclamen and African violets are examples. So, unless as in the case of bromeliads you know that water in their centres is accepted and even needed, try to water the soil and not the centre of the plant.

John Innes Composts

For seed sowing:
- 2 parts by loose bulk medium loam
- 1 part by loose bulk peat
- 1 part by loose bulk sand

To each bushel of this mixture is added:
- $1\frac{1}{2}$ oz. superphosphate of lime
- $\frac{3}{4}$ oz. finely ground chalk or finely ground limestone

For potting:
- 7 parts by loose bulk loam
- 3 parts by loose bulk peat
- 2 parts by loose bulk sand

To each bushel of this mixture is added a fertiliser made up of:
- 2 parts by weight hoof and horn meal
- 2 parts by weight superphosphate of lime
- 1 part by weight sulphate of potash
- $\frac{3}{4}$ oz. finely ground chalk or limestone

J.I. Compost (Potting) No. 1 is made by adding 4 oz. of this fertiliser mixture; No. 2 by adding 8 oz. and No. 3, 12 oz. The chalk content remains the same at $\frac{3}{4}$ oz. for all types. Generally speaking J.I. Potting Compost No. 1 is suitable for all plants, No. 2 for larger and more mature plants and No. 3 for large and vigorous plants.

As a rooting medium for cuttings the John Innes Horticultural Institution recommends a compost made up from:

1 part by loose bulk medium loam
2 parts by loose bulk peat
1 part by loose bulk sand
No fertilisers are added.

CHAPTER V

JUNGLE JARS

My homes in town and country have given house room to jungle jars of the most diverse character!

In my south-facing and therefore sunny, well-windowed London office at present I have a large carboy on one of the desks. It took me quite a time to determine a place for this. The light was not good in the hall, nor was the temperature high enough and under these two conditions the plants in a bottle garden will sicken and die.

In the office it seemed at first as though every place I chose was in the direct line of the sun which shone first through the window and then through the glass of the bottle. If I had allowed this to continue not only would some of the foliage have become scorched, but the heat inside the bottle would have built up to such an extent that the plants would not have been able to survive.

The sun's glare through glass has to be treated with great respect by the indoor gardener. This is why so many plants are most happy when they are grown at right angles to a sunny window. Failing this it is wise to hang a fine curtain to come between the plants and the window glass. This way the light intensity is still good but the danger of burning is eliminated.

There is a great risk also that when a drop of water spills on a plant growing in the sunshine the plant may develop scorch marks. The drop of water acts as a lens and when you consider that it is possible to ignite a piece of paper this way you can realise how a plant can be harmed. Those plants with hairy leaves such as saintpaulias tend to hold droplets of water more easily than others and so must be watered with extreme care.

I finally found a place for my jungle jar on the edge of my desk about 4 feet from the window where the light is good and the sun strikes only fairly early in the day and then not for long. Here the jungle jar has thrived now for some four years and has been a delight and much admired all of that time.

Another carboy of the same size lives on the floor at right angles to the glass door in our cottage living room, against the white wall. In this place it gets no direct sunshine but it is always in good light and it is always in the warm. This jungle jar is three years old.

In London the room temperatures vary more than they do in our country home and sometimes they fall very low and this is one reason why I decided that the town jar should be given more light than the one in the country. The reason for plants 'damping off' and dying in this type of indoor garden is usually because they are kept too dark and too cold at the same time. As a general rule the less the light intensity the more warmth the plants need. But beware of standing a jungle jar too near a source of heat and never place it over a radiator nor on a television set or you will cook it!

In London I also have a copper street lamp with a convenient door, once opened to replace the gas mantles, which allows one to tend the plants easily. Although my first garden in this 'jar' was attractive, it did not live as long as expected. Plants suddenly died of drought in spite of the fact that their roots had been planted in a deep polythene box which fitted snugly into the base of the lamp. This was really surprising, how could the soil have become so dry? On examining the lamp we found that it was not really enclosed as we had thought. A large area hidden by the top portion was open to the air. This was sealed by taping transparent polythene over the open top. The box was replanted and all was well.

When condensation builds up on the inside of the glass as it does sometimes inside tightly closed jars, it is a simple matter to open the lamp door and to wipe the glass dry. It is also possible to keep the door open while the atmosphere dries out a little.

These lamps are not so uncommon and while all may not be made of copper you might be interested enough to search for one and to plant it in the way I have described.

Another and very favourite jungle jar is an outsize brandy balloon type glass which was brought by a visitor as a gift and which has continued to thrive since its arrival. This stands on a low coffee table, again at right angles to a window which in this case faces north. The light is good and very even and there is never any direct sunlight. This jungle jar is filled with cryptanthus and the interesting thing is that it is made from smoke-tinted glass. This appears to have made no difference to the way in which the plants grow. Perhaps they prefer it?

Recently and very reluctantly I had to dismantle a jungle jar which had been growing happily for some four years. Indeed, so well had it done that some of the plants were coming out of the top of the jar! This was the result of an experiment which was so successful that it seems worth passing on.

Someone gave me a packet of mixed cacti and succulent seed and I decided to see what would happen if I sowed the seed directly in a jar. For the purpose I chose a type which is very difficult to fill with plants, a narrow-necked gallon wine jar. The seeds germinated with surprising speed and grew into a most interesting collection which became, as one might expect, rather crowded but always full of interest. Most of the time one peered in at the plants and wondered which one was ultimately going to win. Finally it was one of the succulents, a bryophyllum, and when it finally came out through the mouth of the jar I decided to empty it and begin again.

Incidentally, jars in which seeds are sown should be covered or corked until the seeds germinate.

Still another attractive jungle jar I had was when I decided to use a Victorian glass dome complete with base. I found a bowl that sat easily on this base leaving room to take the dome over it. It was then planted with a selection of small ferns and mossy stones to make a grotto and it proved to be one of the most delightful of all the glassed-in gardens I have had.

From time to time, often to give away to friends, I have made jungle jars in a variety of containers. They have all been enchanting, all have that essential touch of mystery and I recommend the exercise both as a challenging task and a fascinating home decoration.

I have seen carboys filled with happily growing plants which are also the base of a lamp. If you wish to use yours this way you will find that the plants benefit from the slight extra warmth generated by the lamp as well as from its light.

Let us just look back briefly at the history of bottle gardens, because this will help us understand how they work so far as the plants are concerned. It all began with Doctor Nathaniel Bagshaw Ward, who lived from 1791 to 1868. He devised the case which came to be named after him, the Wardian case, in order to transport delicate plants over long distances by land and sea. This was at a time when plant collecting was at its most interesting and lucrative height. It was essential that plants found at such peril to life and limb (let alone the expense involved!) should arrive back safely to be cultivated in the country from which the money poured out to finance the expeditions.

So Dr. N. B. Ward came up with the answer. He made a glass box, timber based, almost hermetically sealed but with a removable top so that the plants could easily be packed. Very few ventilation holes were provided. A plunge bed of damp soil or coconut fibre was installed within the box and the plants in pots, carefully and firmly secured in place, were placed in this. The box was sealed and the plants were left to travel, by bearer or ox-cart, down rivers and across oceans, safe in their own little climate. The Wardian case proved to be a success. So much so in fact that it was not long before improved and more elegant versions came to be made, handsome and splendid enough to occupy an important place in the drawing room and to be filled, you may be sure, with unusual, rare and striking plants.

Some of these Victorian Wardian cases still

exist; I saw one not long ago. As you would expect, genuine originals are now collectors' pieces. Perhaps one day someone will design some on modern lines that will look well in present-day homes. Until then we must make do with what we call jungle jars.

Like the containers for our bowl or dish gardens, the only limit on selection is really that of practicality. If you can possibly lower the plants into the jar and if they have enough room to grow once inside, then the 'jar' can be used. In the spectacular showroom of Rochford's in Hoddesdon there is an enormous bottle lying on its side and filled with beautiful plants instead of the expected sailing ship in full rig.

Although I intend to describe a variety of plants which can be grown together, I hasten to say that there is no reason why more than one plant should be used. One of the little jungle jars that pleased my family as much as any other we have had was a little brandy balloon type glass which held one little fern growing on a carpet of 'bun' moss. This grew quite happily in a north facing window at the top of the stairs.

Usually jars are of clear glass, although I myself have grown plants in light brown, light blue and green tinted jars simply because they happened to be at hand. As I said earlier, one of my jungle jars is doing splendidly in spite of its smoke-tinted glass. Certainly the glass should not only be clean when the jar is first planted, but it should also be kept clean. Cleaning a second-hand jar can sometimes be a lengthy business. I have found that the best method, if the aperture is narrow, is to pour in coarse sand or gravel and soft (preferably rain) water and to keep swirling this around until all the dirt has been coaxed off the sides. After this the jar should be cleaned of the sand or gravel and finally allowed to dry completely inside. If you don't do this you will have such a problem cleaning the glass after the jar has been planted because the soil will stick to the damp sides.

As with the dish gardens a drainage layer is essential. Usually small pebbles or pea gravel is used, but whatever you do, do not pour this into the jar straight on to the glass base or you may break or crack it. First place a thin layer of peat on the floor of the jar to cushion the impact or tilt the jar on its side so that the stones can be inserted more gently. A funnel or cylindrical chute of newspaper or card will be helpful. Insert this well into the neck of the jar if it is as deep as a carboy. First chute in the peat and then the gravel and after this add a few nuggets of charcoal.

Once again, as with the dish gardens, you can use charcoal alone for this drainage layer. Indeed, I prefer this myself and have used it for most of the jungle jars I have made.

This drainage layer needs to be at least two inches deep for a large carboy and proportionately less for smaller jars. I always use John Innes Potting Compost No. 2 for jungle jars. This should give the plants all the nourishment they will require for their lifetime yet not cause them to grow too rampantly. The amount of soil you use will depend upon the size of the container, but it must be deep enough to take the roots of the plants comfortably. Having calculated how much you will need, take about one third and spread this out on newspaper to dry. Treat the other two thirds differently. Spray this until it is uniformly just moist. Test it by taking up a handful and squeezing it gently. It should just, but only just, hold together in a ball. This damp compost is to form the first layer over the drainage material. The dry compost is to go on top to form the final layer, for this will help to seal in the moisture. If you have the moisture content correct then you should not have to water the jar again for many weeks and you will thus have saved yourself from the danger of over-watering.

The soil should be sloped inside the jar. This will give a larger area for planting than if you made the soil surface level. Some people like to landscape this slope by using pieces of cork bark and driftwood, but here of course one is limited by the size of the aperture of the jar. Sometimes I landscape the interior and sometimes I don't, but it may help to know that I have never known the sloped soil to move after planting.

To make bowl or dish gardens one needs no special tools, indeed hands alone can be sufficient. But when we plant jungle jars the case is altered and we need some very strange tools indeed. As a substitute for a trowel or spade we can use an old kitchen spoon, but its handle will need elongating. To do this lash it firmly to a cane. This spoon will dig the holes for the plant roots quite efficiently but it is not very practical for ramming down the soil over their roots and for this quite the best tool is made from a cotton reel on a cane or a long knitting needle. This makes a neat little rammer with which you can pat the soil around the crown of the plant to ensure that it is well anchored. Plants should always be set firmly in the soil so that the roots can absorb nourishment.

While I am on the subject of tools let me describe another which I find invaluable. This is the spiker I use to pick up fallen leaves and other debris from inside the jar. I make it by taping four pins, points outwards of course, around the end of a cane. They must be well secured. The spiker can also be used to detach a dead leaf from a plant. Push the pins into the leaf and give the cane a twist. If it is really dead it will come away from the plant very easily.

If the aperture of the jar is large enough for you to get your hand in there are really few problems to be encountered, but when you are filling a jar with a narrow neck you have to be both careful and patient.

As I suggested for the dish or bowl gardens, first group your plants in the way you wish to see them displayed in the jar, remembering that the soil is sloped and that this will give an impression of height to those planted at the top of the slope. It is best to begin planting at the base of the slope and to work upwards. First make the hole for the plant's roots with your elongated spoon. Tap the plant from its pot and gently loosen as much soil as you can from its roots without damaging them. The root ball must obviously be small enough to go through the neck of the jar. Hold the plant by the tips of its leaves in such a way that this top portion is also made smaller or narrower, tilt the jar and aim the roots for their home. This is, fortunately, considerably easier than it sounds! Spoon the soil around the rim of the planting hole back over the roots and then ram them gently in with the cotton reel, making sure that all are covered and that the crown of the plant is sitting properly on the soil.

If you intend to use driftwood or bark install these as the planting progresses. Never try to place them in position later as this can cause damage to the roots or dislodge the plants.

After planting the jar will need cleaning inside, for some of the soil particles are almost certain to stick to the sides. One should avoid spraying the interior to clean this as otherwise the soil will be made too moist. I have found recently that a tiny home-made feather duster on a piece of strong wire cut from a coat-hanger is as efficient as anything else I have used or tried to use. The wire can be bent to reach around curving surfaces and should the feathers accidentally touch the plants they will not harm them. Indeed, they can be used to brush soil from the plant leaves should this be necessary as it sometimes is. Use a fine brush, the kind in a child's paintbox to remove any soil adhering to the leaves if this cannot be done with the feather duster.

It is not wise to seal the neck of the jar just in case the delicate balance of plants, moisture, air and warmth has not been successfully struck. In any case very little moisture will escape through the narrow neck. If you find excessive condensation on the glass soon after planting this will indicate that there is too much moisture in the soil and it would be well to wipe the glass to remove some of this rather than allow it to trickle back into the soil. A fine cloth or a tissue tied to the end of a strong wire will be useful here. If you have a jar with a lid or stopper, simply remove this and leave it off for a while to give the garden a chance to dry out a little.

Do not confuse this excessive condensation, where the water runs trickling down in real runnels, with the natural slight condensation which you will find most mornings on the interior of a jungle jar. This is merely a form of overnight dew and is quite natural. If the time comes when you see no condensation at all then this is an indication that the soil needs a little moisture. Apply this not by pouring it through the top of the jar but by very gently spraying the interior glass. This will help to clean the interior at the same time. Do remember that very little water will be needed, ever, and absolutely no fertilisers.

For jungle jars try to select slow growing plants with flexible leaves so that these will not become damaged when they are thrust through the narrow aperture. Don't forget that you can try many plants which are normally a little too delicate for most homes. The glorious codiaeum or croton, for example, which likes warm, moist conditions and hates draughts, responds beautifully to the climate in a jar. In this case the narrow-leaved varieties are preferable. The small species of bromeliads or room pines, and especially the cryptanthus I have already described, are excellent and so many of them are prettily coloured with hints of coral pink.

There are species of sellaginella, a dainty moss-cum-fern-like race of plants which will cover the floor of a jar with an attractive carpet. Avoid using helxine, sometimes called baby's tears, for although you might think that such a tiny leaved plant would be perfect for your purpose, you will find that once it starts growing you will not be able to keep it under control. Other good carpeters are the variegated small-leaved fig, *Ficus radicans variegata*, and the green-leaved species, *Ficus pumila*, also with small but rounded leaves.

Fittonia, calathea, maranta, peperomia, pellea, pilea and pellionia and the lovely *Begonia rex* all have prettily marked leaves and are so useful for colour contrasts, but be sure to select them according to the size of the container. You can grow flowering plants such as African violets and if you do you should regularly and scrupulously spike up any fallen petals to prevent excessive damping off inside the jar. A charming berried plant is *Nertera depressa*, whose little fruits seem to sit like orange beads on green fabric.

Many ferns enjoy this type of garden, especially the frail adiantum or maiden-hair which so dislikes the hot, dry air of our living rooms that it will sometimes curl up and die in a few hours. The dainty, wiry-veined aspleniums, often found growing on walls, are ideal especially for very small jars. There is no reason, of course, why you should not plant your garden with all ferns of some kind or another. However, do not try to grow either *Asparagus plumosus* or *A. sprengeri*, neither of which are true ferns.

Miniature palms such as cocos, phoenix and neanthe grow slowly and add grace and height. So does the little cyperus, a miniature papyrus. The variegated sedge is thin and grass-like both in appearance and habit. Avoid using philodendrons for these grow too well. The closely related scindapsus is better, but this should be kept out of strong sunlight. The glossy green spathiphyllum with its white, arum-like flowers, can be grown in a really large jar.

If you want to grow cuttings, either stem or leaf types according to the type of plant, merely press them into the soil using the tip of a cane. You can first dip their ends in hormone rooting powder if you like, although this is not really necessary.

If you wish to sow seeds, use a closed jar. It is quite a simple matter to tie a piece of transparent plastic over the aperture. You can seal a carboy by placing a child's rubber ball in its mouth. This makes a really effective seal.

FOUR STAGES IN THE PLANTING OF A CARBOY

STAGE ONE

A flower pot is being used as a funnel for the roll of paper through which first peat, then gravel and finally soil is poured on to the floor of the carboy.

STAGE TWO

A hole has been made ready for the root of a carex. Its leaves are drawn up to make the plant as slim as possible before it is lowered through the neck of the carboy.

STAGE THREE

Once placed in position the root must be made firm and the soil round the crown of the plant gently rammed with the end of the stick or some other tool so that the plant is well anchored.

STAGE FOUR

To the left is a maranta. The peperomia has just been lowered in place and two sticks, used like giant tweezers, are being used to get the plant in the centre of the hole and also in its correct position.

THE FINISHED CARBOY

The plants in this carboy consists of ferns in variety. The one on the right is *Pteris biaurita argyraea* and has a white line down the centre of mature fronds. The one in the centre is the crested ribbon fern *P. cretica*. Far left is a ladder fern, *Nephrolepis cordifolia*. Right foreground is the Japanese holly fern, *Cyrtomium falcatum*.

CHAPTER VI

PUDDLE POTS

This is my name for an entertaining and easy way of growing plants, and if this is what you are seeking, then puddle pots are just your cup of tea! In fact the allusion to tea is not so far fetched as it may sound because I have seen some very pretty little puddle pot gardens made in lidless teapots.

Furthermore, if you have never been able to get house plants to grow really well and if you feel that the cause of your failure lies in the way you water them, you might be advised to make a puddle pot and grow your plants in water alone. Paradoxical as it may sound, you will have no watering problems then!

Almost any type of water-tight container will do. Choose something that will suit your room and which is deep enough to hold a good layer of pebbles. These anchor the plants and keep them in place. All that actually sustains them is water and the occasional dose of liquid plant food.

Plants grown this way will never make such large specimens as they might in soil, but their enforced tininess gives them a dainty air. A nice thing about this style of indoor gardening is that you can often give the plant a new role to play. For instance, a puddle pot of *Philodendron scandens*, growing, say, in a little tureen, can be used as a pretty table centre. This is hardly the role to suit the plant when it is growing in a flower pot trained to climb up a cane.

You probably know already that it is possible to remove the tips of certain plants and the leaves of others and to stand these in a little jar of plain water where they will soon root. After this they can be transplanted to a pot of soil and grown in the usual way. This is known as taking stem and leaf cuttings and it is an easy and popular method of propagating many house plants.

I find that while many people know about rooting cuttings in water not so many realise that it is possible to keep plants growing in water all the time. As you might expect, not all plants can be grown in this way, but many can. As a general rule all those that root easily in water will continue to grow in it so long as they are fed from time to time. Do this in the usual way, by adding a little liquid plant food to the rooting medium, in this case water.

You can use either rooted or unrooted cuttings. In either case, when you use stem cuttings see that the portion of stem that is to go under water is stripped of any leaves, otherwise these might rot and turn the water foul.

It is possible, though not necessary, to use a hormone rooting powder to hasten root formation.

From time to time it is a good thing, I think, to aerate a puddle pot, especially in summer when the water may become warm. I do this by taking it to the sink and letting the tap run quite hard into the container. This forces the old water out and recharges the roots with fresh air.

You will find that there is a good enough selection of suitable plants to make this type of gardening worth while.

Bear in mind that plants do not have to be mixed. Puddle pots can be made to contain one kind of plant only.

You will find that when grown in water alone all plants become more finely drawn, their leaves become smaller and daintier and their stems thinner. The philodendron I mentioned earlier will scramble and trail more in the manner of a small ivy than the vigorous aeroid it is normally seen to be. Its effect is much more appealing. You might like to experiment with any other plants which appeal to you. Generally speaking, all those plants which send out aerial roots along their stems will root in water.

If you are interested in flower arrangement you can treat your plant cuttings in much the same way that you would arrange cut blooms and foliage. You can, for example, anchor an attractive piece of driftwood to form the line and backbone of the arrangement and set the various cuttings at its foot. You will then have a decoration which is slowly growing rather than one you can expect to fade.

Remember too that supplementary containers have a use in indoor gardening. You can root or plant cuttings and small plants in small tubes, jars, polythene bags and even party balloons, which can be fastened to and hidden behind the driftwood. Black polythene is very inconspicuous. Plants displayed this way look as though they are actually growing from the wood and they decorate it very effectively. In spring you can use certain little bulb flowers this way too. There are so many attractive ways of displaying plants and growing some of them, simply, in water makes this very easy indeed.

Like many other people I so enjoy a flower arrangement composed entirely of foliage, and puddle pots give me a chance of perpetuating this type of decoration. At the moment of writing I have near me a little sage-green dolphin vase from which rises and cascades all kinds of foliage in a sweet colour harmony. They are all cuttings and all are growing well after just a month. They include rhoicissus, plectranthus, chlorophytum, philodendron, tradescantia and a lovely focal point of coleus, the colours of which harmonise with the undersides of so many of the 'green' leaves.

There is a further point about puddle pots. If ever you wish to dismantle one you can always pot the rooted cuttings individually and let each go on to live a life of its own.

Generally speaking, the shallower the vessel the more heavily you should anchor the plants. Any kind of stones or pebbles will do for a puddle pot. If I have several to make I tend to go out into the drive and pick over the gravel, but at other times I like to search for those stones which have moss

1 A puddle-pot being prepared. Cuttings of existing house plants, left to right, coleus, rhoicissus, Philodendron scandens, plectranthus and chlorophytum in foreground, right. Nearby is charcoal to strew on the base, pebbles to hold the plants, water to fill the pot.

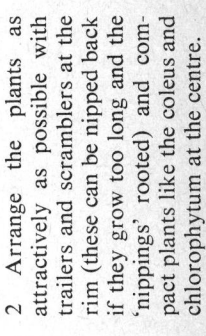

2 Arrange the plants as attractively as possible with trailers and scramblers at the rim (these can be nipped back if they grow too long and the 'nippings' rooted) and compact plants like the coleus and chlorophytum at the centre.

3 When all are in place, stems held as far up as rim level by the pebbles, top up the container with more pebbles or attractive stones of some other kind between the plants. Pour in water so that its level is just below the rim.

growing on them. These will continue to keep beautifully green because the stones, and consequently the moss also are kept constantly moist. I also have some special 'pebbles' I use from time to time.

Although these are used merely to provide a root hold and anchor, I am sure you will realise that in a plant arrangement of this type the pebbles you use can add considerably to both the beauty and the interest of the composition. For instance, a great piece of beautifully shaped coral can be set above the smaller pebbles to form a focal point. Quartz or certain other minerals will add colour. Even coal can be dramatic and decorative. Shells will add colour and also contrasts of texture. Small shells will hold down cuttings and so play both a utilitarian and a decorative role. Larger shells within the puddle pot can anchor and hold cuttings, to give a two-layer garden!

Shells, like any pebbles you may have collected on the seashore, should be boiled or soaked in several changes of water until all the salt has been drawn away, otherwise this will certainly affect the plants.

You will need to fill the vessel to within half an

inch of the brim with pebbles and the water level should be just below their surfaces.

You can use either translucent or opaque containers. Many people like to use glass because they find it interesting to watch the development of the roots. If you do use these do not stand the glass in a sunny window because the light will cause too much bacterial activity in the water and this might become sour. Glass containers are best well back from the light. They can hold those plants which grow in the shadier areas of the home. These include philodendrons, hedera (the green leaved varieties), rhoicissus, plectranthus and syngonium.

If you have the choice it is best first to decide where you would like the puddle pot to stand and then to plan its contents. As I have already suggested, you could consider using this type of decoration as a table centre. If you do then select only those plants which will grow well away from direct light. As a general rule the deeper green the leaf the further from the light it will grow. Variegated plants like more light but not direct sunlight glaring through glass. Avoid standing a puddle pot in any place where the water could become heated.

To make stem cuttings cut all shoots just below a joint or node, remove the lower leaves from the portion likely to be under water, insert the stem in the water and wedge it firmly in place with one or more pebbles.

If you use leaf cuttings see that the lower part of the blade of the leaf near the stem is also under water.

Once the roots have started to grow and explore the spaces between the pebbles you should give the plants a little fertiliser once a month. Make this very weak at first. It is better to give too little of this than too much. Be sure to keep the water level topped up frequently.

Although cuttings do so well, your choice for components of a puddle pot does not have to be limited to them alone, for you can also use many plants. For example, cyperus and carex which are best propagated by division, both like moist, swampy conditions in their natural surroundings. These will grow well after root washing and so will many ferns. In spring I have often treated many simple wild plants such as daisies from the lawn, primroses, violets and celandines this way and they grow and bloom quite well. I lift them when they are in bud. Once they have flowered they begin to fade, but can easily be replaced.

For a kitchen you can grow parsley this way.

The thing to do with any plant is first to wash the soil carefully from the roots. When planting spread these out and place the pebbles on them until the plant is secured. Don't forget to strew a good quantity of charcoal on the floor of any container you use to keep the water sweet.

The pretty little *Saxifraga sarmentosa*, sometimes called Mother of Thousands, produces long stolons or runners at the ends of which tiny plants grow. These will root fastest when they are still attached to the parent plant. You can always induce a runner or a layer to root into its own small puddle pot and transplant it to the main pot later on. Baby chlorophytums are best rooted this way.

If you do not consider yourself 'plant death' (which is what a friend of mine calls herself) and instead of killing plants are surrounded by those which thrive and grow abundantly, then you will have a wonderful source from which you can collect plants for your pebble planters. Nip out young and well-shaped tips of stems.

If you are beginning from scratch you may

have to beg from your friends. It might be that you will have to begin in a modest way with just one or two cuttings and then add to your pebble planter from time to time. Fortunately this is quite feasible. Build up your collection as you would a painting or a piece of needlework and add to it as the opportunity occurs. You cannot harm the existing plants, for it is a simple matter merely to insert another one or two in some other part of the planter, and you can pile pebbles one on the other, for the roots will find their own way through them.

Old but attractive teapots make surprisingly good containers, for they offer a good depth of water, no wide aperture or surface from which it can quickly evaporate and a handle by which the planter can easily be held if and when it has to be moved. You will find also that once the plants begin to grow they will flow quite prettily over the edge and disguise the ledge where the lid usually sits.

This flowing also goes for all other containers and where low dishes of all kinds look well, I think that those that are raised on a pedestal look even better for this style of garden.

Flower vases, particularly urns, are good, and

these also, like the teapot, offer a good depth of water. There is nothing, I hasten to add, against shallow containers from the point of view of the plants, but there is on the practical side. In the first place all puddle pots have to be moved from time to time if only to dust around them and it is all too easy to spill water from a shallow container. Then there is the character of the plants to consider. So many of the water-rooters are spreaders and sprawlers and growing in a low container they tend to sit on the table surface and become disarranged or even damaged when they are moved. They look much better when seen pendant.

Converting them into puddle pots is an attractive way of dressing up some gifts. Let me explain. Suppose you found a little piece of old china for a friend, say a cup and saucer, a shaving mug, a moustache cup or any of the pleasantly decorated domestic china that collectors love. If you fill it with little plants before you pass it on your friend can have the pleasure both of enjoying the china and watching the plants grow. Should he or she wish to separate one from the other then the rooted cuttings can be potted up in the usual way and so you would have passed on also the beginnings of a little plant collection as well as an addition to the china cupboard.

These pebble planters make delightful gifts and one of the advantages of making them for this purpose is that you do not have to begin months and months ahead. Indeed, once you know which plants can be relied on to root and grow you can even assemble a garden at the last moment. Obviously it is best to have the cuttings rooted before you pass them on, if only for your own peace of mind. Much will depend on where or to whom the little garden is to go.

Containers can be varied. Pebble planters can be either shallow or deep. For in this case you are not concerned with finding sufficient room for the root balls of several plants. You can, if you wish, select containers of an entirely different character from those you would choose for bowl gardens.

Vessels associated with liquids naturally spring first to mind and are very attractive when filled. This is a delightful way, for instance, to use a giant cup and saucer, a deep sugar basin or a water jug. Polythene lined copper kettles and saucepans, pretty on the kitchen window when filled with plants, and other attractive kitchen utensils may be employed. For wall decoration you can use a warming pan with a container for the plants secured inside just under the lid.

Before we leave puddle pots, just a word or two about other plants which offer a little diversion, especially if there are children in the family. In my chapter on bulbs you will discover that many bulbs can be grown this way and I thoroughly recommend this method.

You can also grow a 'vine' from a potato. In this case you will need the pebbles in a deep glass jar with water coming almost to the top, a large preserving jar will do quite well. 'Plant' the potato on and among the pebbles, eyes-end uppermost, so that it is half in and half out of the pot with its buried end not quite touching the water. The plant can become very heavy, so make sure to anchor it well. Don't forget to put a little charcoal in the water. Now stand it in the light and wait for results. I have seen such splendid potato plants grown both in puddle pots and in plain water. The roots even develop tiny potatoes in time!

You can use this method also for a sweet potato, for this is the root of a true vine or climber. Make sure though that it has not been kiln dried first, as some are that reach this country. Avocados and all kinds of large seeds such as conkers, sweet chestnuts and butter beans can also be grown.

I have before now planted all these things, including a tiny potato among other plants in puddle pots. They are surprisingly attractive and usually puzzle one's guests.

An avocado stone can be grown in the same manner as the potato, although it will not produce tubers of course. It makes a good plant but can become tiresome because it tends after a while to grow lopsided or to develop a long bare stem. This is natural enough, for after all an avocado is a tree in its natural environment.

Many readers write to ask me when they can expect their avocado plant to produce fruit. I am afraid that the answer is that it won't, at least not when grown under home conditions. This is because in the first place it has to develop into a tree before it is mature enough to produce fruit and secondly even then the sexes are on separate plants and there is no way of telling until it flowers which sex the potted plant is likely to be.

Children are fascinated by puddle pots and there are many short-term plants they can grow to make it all so much more fun. Added to the spring plants I mentioned earlier there is also Creeping

Jenny, or *Lysimachia nummularia*, from which it is quite easy to pull the odd stem with a few roots attached. These will increase in water. If you can find some way of suspending the puddle pot the Creeping Jenny shoots can be made to grow like a hanging basket which in summer will become studded with the pretty yellow flowers. This is a plant for a shady window, not full sun. Leafy shoots of nasturtium will also root and continue to grow in water.

When you prepare carrots, turnips, radish, swedes and parsnips, and a beetroot too if you are going to cube it for soup, cut a thick slice from the top so that you take off the crown with sufficient root tissue to sustain it. All of these tops will grow into little plants. If you have it, first strew a little sand over the floor of the pot. This will help keep the slices in place. You can then arrange the pebbles around them.

CHAPTER VII

NATURE'S PREPACKS

Inside every bulb you buy is a potential flower! Packed into that plump, round shape is the little plant just waiting for you to provide the right conditions to make it grow. And growing bulbs is a wonderful form of indoor gardening. You can grow bulbs if you have only one room and you can grow them for many months on end, spreading the flowers over autumn, winter and spring.

All you have to do is to find the right way to grow the bulbs. Wrongly cultivated, the potentially lovely flower will emerge stunted and unhappy, but properly cared for the flowers will grow to be the most beautiful things you have ever seen. And it is all so easy, really.

Spring-flowering bulbs need a taste of winter before they can flower. In some cases the bulb merchants give them this by storing them for predetermined periods in low temperatures and when bulbs have been specially treated in this manner they are usually sold as 'prepared' bulbs. Not all will accept the cool store treatment, but those that will are also those bulbs that will flower earliest, even at Christmas. So if you want to be certain of having flowers then you should buy the 'specially prepared' kinds, which may cost just a little more. Among these, hyacinths are the most responsive and the most popular.

Those others that have not been specially prepared by the merchant have to be given a spell of winter by the person who grows them. In the home the easiest way to do this is to find some place which is both cold and dark and to store the planted bulbs there until they are ready to force into early bloom. Commercial growers plunge the pots and bowls outside and bury them deep under several inches of ashes or some other plunge medium. Some home gardeners do this too, but I find it a bit of a nuisance. Furthermore, you can't bury precious bowls because they may become stained or damaged and I do like to arrange my bulbs in attractive containers. So I use a simpler, less fussy and cleaner method. I wrap each bowl of bulbs in either black polythene or several thicknesses of heavy brown paper. (It's surprising how much black polythene one can save during the year!) Then I stand these wrapped bowls on the ground, sometimes if I have several, one is straddled over the other on the north side of the house. In London I place them out on my roof garden. They can also go on the window-sill outside or on a balcony, in the cellar, under the roof, in a shed or a cold spare room, anywhere, in fact, where the temperature will be lower than it is in the living room. As you can see, this is really all quite simple and for me it has been successful each year except for one time when some field mice found the *Crocus chrysanthus* and ate them. This taught me to open my parcels and inspect the bulb bowls frequently.

This, then, is the first and most important rule. All the spring flowering bulbs, and by spring I mean any time after the shortest day, must be kept cool and dark in their early stages. During this 'winter' period the bulbs will develop their roots and until these are well grown and ready both to feed and anchor the rest of the plant we cannot possibly successfully force the leaves and flowers to grow quickly. If you do try to hurry the bulbs before their roots are ready, stunted leaves and undeveloped flowers will result.

Not all of the November and December flowering bulbs have to be prepared. For some of them it is their natural flowering time, luckily for us. The dainty Roman hyacinths will flower as early as November without forcing. This charming little flower is white, fragrant and loosely growing, with only a few bells to each stem, but it makes up for this by having several stems to a bulb. The bulbs, by the way, are also very small, especially when compared with the larger-flowered hyacinths so don't think that you have a poor sample.

Planted in September, Roman hyacinths should flower by Christmas. If you would like them for November, so often a bleak and barren month where little flowers are concerned, plant the bulbs in August. Planted in October you can have them in flower for January. So you can have a succession if you like.

If you prefer coloured flowers to white, pink Rosalie is a Roman type miniature hyacinth and Vanguard is a light blue miniature which can easily be forced into flower by the middle of December. As a rule small flowered hyacinths other than the Roman are known as multi-flowering because of their habit of sending up several spikes from one bulb. They are all sweetly scented.

Also flowering easily and naturally at the end of winter are some of the narcissi. Paper White Grandiflora is an important name for those little shilling sized white narcissi which grow in fragrant bunches on the ends of long stems. These are the only bulbs which can be placed directly on a window-sill after being planted. They grow very tall and sometimes flop over if they are not anchored properly, so try to provide deep containers for them so that they can send their roots down deeply. I grow these in pebbles and water.

Similar in habit but a bright golden yellow is Grand Soleil d'Or. Coming close on the heels of these two varieties is one of my favourites, the narcissus poetaz Cragford. The stems carry four- or five-clustered flowers which have white perianths (petals) and vivid orange-scarlet cups. They are also beautifully scented. This is another fine variety to grow in pebbles. Geranium, orange and white, and Scarlet Gem, red and green on white, are two other beauties. Plant them in early August if you can, for really early blooms.

First after these to come into flower are the lovely exhibition hyacinths, those great, heavy, flower-studded spikes with the heavenly perfume. These will need to be planted early in September if you want them to flower for Christmas, and for these earliest flowers you will need prepared bulbs. The unprepared kinds flower later, and if you plant these early enough they will be sufficiently developed by Christmas to be used as gifts.

If you care to plant a bowl of bulbs every week for a couple of months you can ensure a house full of gay flowers from Christmas onwards, earlier if you choose carefully.

There is so much to say about growing bulbs indoors and also about what kinds and what varieties to grow that it is difficult for me to know where to begin! So I will start where I began, as a little girl growing a hyacinth bulb in plain water.

In those days there seemed always to be rows of hyacinth glasses on sale in the windows of ironmongers and stores and I seem to remember a hyacinth growing in a glass in every window in the street with even more along the window-sills. Once I had grown up and wished to start growing the bulbs again the glasses had disappeared! For some years it became so difficult to buy them that

I and many more people took to growing the bulbs in preserving jars and similar domestic containers. Now hyacinth glasses are coming back again, although many are different in design and not necessarily made of glass. The old types are there though for the searching, and I for one never pass an antique shop if I see one on sale in the window.

Sometimes you can find tiny glasses made on the same principle, a bowl shaped portion at the top in which the bulb sits snugly and a fairly large and deep portion under this to take the roots. You can grow crocuses, scillas and Roman hyacinths this way, and although they are not bulbs, acorns! Little glass bottles, jars, paste pots, cold cream jars and mustard glasses are just a few other receptacles which will take some of these smaller bulbs or corms.

When you grow any bulb in water you need a little nugget of charcoal in the water to keep it sweet. Always make sure that the bulb or corm is sitting really firmly in the top of the glass, for once it begins to grow it will become heavy and if it is not held properly it may topple over and become damaged. No more than the very base of the bulb or corm should be touching the water.

Try to use rainwater if you can, for this is so much better for the plant.

Keep the glasses in a cool place at the beginning. If this is not also dark, then cover the bulbs. You can cover them individually if you wish by making little clown's caps of brown paper large enough to go over the bulb and the glass. Let them remain cool and dark until you see the roots growing from the base of the bulb down into the water. You can then take off the cap and watch events. Continue to keep the glass in a fairly cool place, a shady window rather than a sunny one for example, until the flower spikes begin to show and to colour. Always turn the pots a quarter turn each day to ensure that they grow evenly. Keep the water topped up when necessary.

This really is an easy and fascinating way of growing hyacinths!

From plain water it is not a great step to water and pebbles. In our last chapter we saw how many plants can be grown in puddle pots, so perhaps it is not surprising that many bulbs will also grow this way. The method seems to suit narcissi in particular. Any of those varieties which a bulb merchant recommends for indoor growing or forcing is almost certain to grow well in pebbles.

A good catalogue will list varieties. Incidentally, all narcissi should be planted in late August and early September. If you delay planting results may be disappointing. As in the puddle pot gardens, the pebbles are used as anchorage for the numerous roots.

Using this method planting the bulbs is very simple. First place a little charcoal on the floor of a deep bowl. Fill to within 2 inches of the brim with pebbles. Sit the bulbs on this. They can be quite close together but they should not be touching. You will find that the 'noses' of the bulbs are well above the bowl rim, and this is how it should be.

Next arrange the pebbles around the bulbs so that they are well supported by them and they all sit firmly. Pour in the rainwater so that its level is just under the surface of the pebbles. Place the bowls in a cool dark place until the roots are running well. This is usually between five and eight weeks according to the type of bulb being grown. You can soon see if the roots are growing by moving a few pebbles.

You can grow hyacinths in pebbles too if you wish.

The next simple medium in which to grow

bulbs is bulb fibre, with which almost everyone is familiar. It is simply six parts of loose peat, two parts of oyster shell and and one part of crushed charcoal, all well mixed together and thoroughly moistened before the bulbs are planted in it.

Its value lies in the fact that the peat retains moisture yet is loose enough to permit the roots to range through it and to anchor the plants as though they were in soil. The use of the oyster shell is probably traditional, for coarse sand would serve the same purpose. Charcoal, as you know, keeps the medium sweet.

This mixture contains no nourishment. You will find that an occasional light feed with some liquid manure or plant food during their growing period will keep the bulb's foliage really dwarf and impart a good colour to the flowers.

Bulb fibre suits many bulbs, certainly all those which will grow in water or pebbles and water. But many others such as double early tulips will grow better in fibre although most other tulips prefer soil. Incidentally, you should take care to see that the bulb fibre never dries out, which it is apt to do in a warm, dry atmosphere or when put away in the cool and forgotten.

Levington compost may be used instead of bulb

fibre. Leafmould or soil can also be used to plant all bulbs, but it is probable here that some weeds will also grow. Some people believe in half filling the bowl with leafmould and then topping up with fibre. This can be a good idea if you can easily get leafmould and if the budget is tight. Indoor bulbs grown in soil are most likely to flower in the garden the following year. When soil is used make a good drainage layer in the bowl or alternatively use flower pots instead of bowls.

All bulbs can be planted in the garden when they are finished indoors, although it is best to wait until any really severe weather has passed. While they are awaiting transplanting in this way the bulbs should be watered and cared for.

Tulips are not quite so easy to grow in a home as the other flowers I have mentioned, mainly, I think, because they are expected to settle in quickly to the warmth and light of the average home and this they cannot do. If you would like to grow tulips, try first with the double early varieties which will grow very well in fibre and even better in one of the soil-less composts such as Levington.

These bulbs have large, sweet-smelling blooms. Both the perfume and the flower's shape are reminiscent of the rose. In fact one variety is actually called Tearose. There are several lovely varieties ranging in colour from white through yellow to orange, pink and deep red. Nearly all double early tulips are suitable for forcing.

The early singles are more plentiful and there are very many from which you can make your choice. Many have a delicious fragrance. They flower nice and early and are comparatively easy to grow.

Personally I would advise you to concentrate on these two types of tulips for indoor growing and to ignore the later, taller kinds. Some of these will force, but they are not easy for any but the skilled cultivator.

The best time to plant tulips is in September and October. Do not attempt to force any planted after this date. Tulips other than the earlies I have described do best in good soil mixed with sand and leafmould, or alternatively in J.I. Potting Compost.

Do not expect any of the tulips to flower by Christmas. You may be lucky but such luck is rare when these plants are being grown under home conditions. They may reach the bud stage though.

Since it is easy to make mistakes, let us concentrate for the moment on just what the pattern of cultivation should be. I have already stressed that the essential factor is that the bowls and pots should be stored in a cold and dark place until the roots are well formed and the leaves actually growing out of the top of the bulbs.

While they are in store do not forget to inspect your bulbs at least once a week to ensure that the fibre or soil is still moist. If this dries the roots will shrivel and this will be fatal. Even those bowls wrapped and placed out of doors may also dry out after a time, although those wrapped in plastic are more likely to keep moist for weeks. But be sure also to inspect these.

You will probably find that no water is needed for the first two weeks. Don't neglect the hyacinth glasses and pebble bowls. Remember that Cragford and other narcissi grown in fibre rather than in pebbles should be kept very moist at the roots during this time.

Hyacinths ought not to be brought out before they have had at least eight weeks in the cool and dark. Tulips take ten to twelve weeks before they are brought out. These should be 3–4 inches high, and even then for the first few days they should be protected from the light by covering them lightly with sheets of paper. Narcissi vary from five to eight weeks according to the variety and type. You can get a guide from the shoots, which should be about 4 inches tall with the flower bud well out of the neck of the bulb. Crocuses must be almost ready to flower.

Once the shoots are well away the bowls can be brought into a warmer and lighter atmosphere but they should not be placed straight away in sunny windows or in a warm living room. Remember also that you don't have to bring them all out at the same time. Make a succession. They will come to no harm if left in the cool and dark for a little longer. If you must move them, however, find another place which is light but cool. The plants must be introduced to their forcing temperature very slowly. Put them in the coolest part of your home to begin with and as the flower buds begin to grow, as they become plumper and more and more conspicuous, the bowls can be moved just as gradually into warmer conditions. As one bowl moves from one zone to another bring in one more to take its place.

Incidentally, a shady window-sill not over a radiator seldom gets really warm in winter, so this can be a good place to stand bulbs in their early stages. Wherever they stand, give them all a quarter turn each day to keep them growing evenly.

I really do think that the truly important thing is not to be impatient. It is just impossible to hasten these early steps successfully and if you try to do so then failure is assured. This goes for all types of bulbs.

Be sure to water them. Surprising as it may seem, I find that people do forget to do this once the bulbs come out into the light. But it is just as important at this stage as earlier. The plants will now be growing more rapidly and will need plenty of water. However, less water will be necessary once the bulbs are in bloom. Do not pour water over the bulbs themselves, instead water the surface of the fibre or soil.

It is not really good to try to grow mixtures of bulbs. They seldom grow at the same rate, so keep one kind together. I do like to mix them with other plants though, and just as I do when making dish gardens I often plant an empty flower pot or two in a bowl. The bulbs are set around this and while they are in store their roots grow, avoiding the pot area. When the containers are brought out and into the home as decoration the empty pot is easily removed without causing any damage to the roots. It is then replaced by some plant which will complement the flowers.

When the bulbs are fading they are not attractive but they should still be cared for indoors until the foliage has died down. If you have several bowls you will not want them cluttering up the place, so why not take a leaf from the outdoor gardener's book. Lift your bulbs and transplant them to some other place. Once the frosts have finished you can plant them in the garden, but until then make a temporary 'bed' from a deep box. Lift the faded bulbs from their bowls, pack them in rows in the box carefully dividing them into kinds and varieties by labels or strips of polythene. You can pack them quite tightly for this brief ripening period.

Bear in mind that you cannot force them again the following year but they will live to flower again in the garden, although it may take them a year or two to recover. If you cut the foliage you will delay them further. Just let it die down naturally and when it turns brown and comes away with the merest tug it can be removed. The bulbs can then be stored until autumn or planted in the garden right away.

A BOWL GARDEN

A bowl containing a few narcissi bulbs, later forced in the usual way in the bowl, had spaces left at planting time to take other bulbs and plants when the narcissi were ready to be brought out of the dark. They include snowdrops, London pride, left; primroses at the centre and to the right in front of the crocuses. A few trails of ivy flow over the rim and through the narcissi.

CHAPTER VIII

REJUVENATING, REPLANTING AND DOCTORING

When I plant my bowl and dish gardens I often plant an empty flower pot among the plants and you may remember that I suggested doing this when you plant bulbs. The reason for doing so when I mix plants is so that I can easily give my little garden a new look from time to time.

Most of the plants we grow are those favoured for the beauty or the interest of their foliage and I think that it often improves a little garden greatly to include a floral focal point of some kind. As flowering plants as a general rule are not so long lasting as the foliage kinds, one needs to have some method of being able to replace them easily and quickly. So if when assembling your leafy tenants you also plant an empty 3-inch pot, or perhaps a larger size for a larger garden, then all you have to do is to remove the empty flower pot and replace it with a full one when you find the flowering plant you like. Alternatively, if you begin with a flowering plant in a pot it is a simple matter to remove a shabby plant and substitute a fresher one.

Most of the flowering plants on sale are out of their normal flowering season and for this reason they do not last as long as otherwise they might. Another factor against a long life is that they are brought into the highly artificial conditions of our living rooms which are nothing like so humid as the greenhouses in which they were raised. Personally I think that one must be philosophical about this and look on flowering pot plants in the same way as cut flowers, as expendable items not expected to live for ever, but meanwhile offering up a little prayer of thanks because they do last a little longer!

Some flowering plants, azaleas, primulas and heathers for example, are likely to need a great deal more water than the foliage plants surrounding them. In this case I always slip the flower pot into a small, watertight polythene bag. The flowering plant can then be watered as much as necessary without danger of making the surrounding soil sodden and killing the others.

Along the same lines, there is no reason why you should not liven up a dish garden, especially if it is looking a little tired after a long soft winter in a warm, dry room, by using cut flowers. In this case, instead of an empty flower pot you need some little waterproof vessel such as a yoghurt container. This is a pretty way to use spring flowers such as posies of aconites, snowdrops, crocuses and primroses.

Do not mix them in their bunches though, for you will not get such an attractive effect as you will do if you mass one kind together. Use them to make separate knots of colour.

In the same way you can lift flowering or budding bulbs from the garden and pack them inside an empty flower pot. If you have no garden you might find it worth while to grow a few extra bulbs in boxes for this purpose. You will not need many to transform a dish garden and you can so easily plan a succession so that you can maintain a steady show of new flowers about the house.

It is really surprising how long little indoor gardens (and large ones too, come to that!) can remain looking lovely and fresh. This is really up to you. As I said earlier, plants respond to an occasional spray with clean tepid water over the foliage, for this not only gives them the extra moisture so essential to some but it is also a very good way of keeping their leaves free from dust. However, one should take care that this is not done in rooms that are too cool in winter.

But one does not have to be concerned only with tidiness. There is the danger, of course, that plants will outgrow their environment and plants that were once compact and neat will become leggy, untidy and perhaps discoloured. When a plant is being grown singly in a pot it is possible easily to tell if it needs repotting, that is, to be moved on to a pot one size larger, merely by knocking it from its pot and examining its root system. If you see the roots coiled evenly around the outside of the mass known as the root ball, showing that they are in fact running round the inside wall of the pot, then it is time that the plant is moved on. But of course it is not so easy to do this when a community of plants are growing together. In the first place not all the plants will grow at the same rate. Even so, I have moved an entire bowl garden to a larger container just in the same way as I repot a plant.

More generally, however, it seems to be just one or two plants which need changing rather than all. When a plant has to go it is best to prise it up from the mass rather as you would dig up a plant from the garden. You can use a kitchen fork quite effectively for this. The plant can then be potted up and given a chance to recuperate before you use it in another mixture, should this be your plan.

Incidentally, take care that you do not move the plant to a pot which is really too large for it. Remember that it has been living under crowded conditions and that it will not relish a too sudden switch to a great deal of root room. Choose a pot which will give about half an inch all round extra space.

If you want the plants to grow very slowly as they must in jungle jars, then it would not be wise either to give them a very rich soil mixture to grow in or to feed them continually. On the other hand certain plant foods are vital to the good health of a plant.

The three main plant foods are nitrogen, phosphates and potassium. All are necessary but some plants require more of one than another. The proprietary plant foods available to us commercially are what are called 'balanced' so far as house plants are concerned and this means that their proportions suit all plants on the average.

Nitrogen promotes lush, green growth. Phosphates help the establishment of a strong root system and give strength and ripeness to a plant. Potash helps plants to build up reserves of strength and food inside themselves. Trace elements and many minerals are necessary to plant health but in such minute quantities that they are not generally considered in foods for house plants with their comparatively small requirements of soil.

There is very little to choose between the various brands of house plant foods available. Read the directions on the packet or bottle very carefully and never make the mistake of being too generous or you will kill your plants.

Fortunately all house plants are relatively clear of all pests and diseases. This is due to two main reasons. In the first place the nurseries which produce our plants must take every precaution to avoid these troubles in order to maintain good crops and therefore good profits, so it is very rarely indeed that a new plant will bring its own pest or disease with it. Secondly, our homes are normally cleaned often enough to get rid of any pests that may fly in through the windows and maintained in a state which also prevents the growth of fungoid diseases.

One of the most aggravating of pests is a tiny mite known as red spider and this attacks only when the atmosphere is dry and warm. Yellowing of the leaves followed by browning and dropping are the signs to look for and a close examination will reveal a very fine web on some of the leaves although the actual mite itself is usually too small to be seen. Spraying the affected plant or dipping it completely (except the pot) in a suitable insecticide will clear this pest, but if it gets a good hold it is really better to get rid of the plant entirely.

Aphids, mainly greenfly, so familiar in our gardens, sometimes come into the house through an open window or on flowers brought in from the garden. These are easily enough seen and killed, using preferably one of the several good systemic insecticides available. Remember that all sprays are of necessity more or less poisonous, so use them with great care, preferably out of doors.

Mealy bugs and scale insects look respectively like little pieces of fluff and like tiny woodlice. Both are best handled individually, using a matchstick or something similar dipped in insecticide to remove and kill them. They are seldom seen in great colonies simply because they do not get the time to breed as they are easily discovered.

As with all pests and diseases prevention is better than cure and if plants are raised in a comparatively humid atmosphere and kept clean and well fed it is most unlikely that any severe infestation will ever occur.

Domestic gas, even in the most minute quantities, will kill some plants including African violets, pelargoniums, begonias and cyclamen. Even a gas water heater in another room can cause great damage. Fumes from oil heaters will also kill some plants. Signs of distress are yellowing leaves.

Heating can be as dangerous to some plants as cold is to others, particularly if the air is dry. Never allow any plants too near any source of heat. Draughts, either hot or cold, can cause great damage.

The humidity necessary to nearly all plants is only beneficial if the plants can breathe through their pores. If these are clogged with dust and dirt the plants will choke. Keep leaves clean by gently wiping large ones with a soft, damp tissue (never oil, milk or anything else to get a good shine on them) and by spraying plants with smaller leaves.

One of the best things you can do for a house plant is to put it outside in a gentle summer shower.

Guard against frosts if your plants live on a window-sill, for most rooms cool off somewhat at night and the frost can strike through the glass. Bring them into the room at night when you go to bed if you have a really cold spell.

Normal mists of moist air do plants no harm but a dark industrial fog or smog can actually kill plants. Keep doors and windows closed so far as is possible and if things are really bad you may be able to save some plants by sealing them in polythene bags for a few days.

These bags can also be useful to keep plants moist while you are away on holiday. Water the plants well first and seal the bags tightly after first blowing into them to keep the sides clear of plant leaves. Keep these miniature greenhouses in good light but not in a position where the sun could strike them for more than a few minutes at a time.

Better still if you are going away during the summer months, is to place your house plants in a shaded place in the garden, plunging the pots in moist peat to keep the roots cool. But remember that outdoors they may be attacked by slugs and aphids. So put down slug pellets and spray with a systemic insecticide and when you return the plants should be all the better for their own little holiday in the open air.

CORGI MINI-BOOKS

☐	76359 4	FAVOURITE RECIPES	15p
☐	76055 2	BEAUTY AND YOU Elizabeth Anderson	12½p
☐	76050 1	HAIRCARE Elizabeth Anderson	15p
☐	76047 1	YOGA POCKET TEACHER Russell Atkinson	15p
☐	76353 5	HOME MOVIES Robert Bateman	15p
☐	76317 9	TEACH YOUR OWN CHILD Madeleine Bingham	12½p
☐	76329 2	A CAREER FOR YOUR DAUGHTER Madeleine Bingham	12½p
☐	76358 6	WOOLCRAFTS Caroline Brandt	15p
☐	76098 6	THE YOUTH SECRET Barbara Cartland	15p
☐	76344 6	THE MAGIC OF HONEY Barbara Cartland	15p
☐	76071 4	WRITING—THE EASY WAY Hunter Diack	12½p
☐	76042 0	NO TIME TO COOK BOOK Hilda Finn	12½p
☐	76362 4	THE WORLD IN YOUR SAUCEPAN Hilda Finn	15p
☐	76320 9	THE VITAL YOU Kenneth Gee	12½p
☐	76314 4	COINS—A COLLECTOR'S GUIDE Elizabeth Gilzean	12½p
☐	76041 2	HOBBIES FOR WOMEN Elizabeth Gilzean	12½p
☐	76073 0	LOOKING AFTER YOUR TROPICAL AQUARIUM John Graham	12½p
☐	76095 1	FLOWER ARRANGEMENT Sarah Haddon	12½p
☐	76313 6	FISHING—THE ANGLER'S GUIDE Brian Harris	12½p
☐	76094 3	LOOKING AFTER YOUR CAGED BIRD Nick Henderson	12½p
☐	76093 5	LOOKING AFTER YOUR CAT Nick Henderson	15p
☐	76327 6	LET'S GO TO THE ZOO Nick Henderson	12½p
☐	76326 8	GIVING PARTIES Katherine Howard	12½p
☐	76075 7	AMATEUR PHOTOGRAPHY Sean Jennett	12½p
☐	76078 1	GAMES AND PLAY FOR THE SICK CHILD George and Cornelia Kay	15p
☐	76074 9	INDOOR PLANTS Kenneth Lemmon	12½p
☐	76360 8	WINTER GARDENS Kenneth Lemmon	15p
☐	76348 9	WINDOW BOX AND TUB GARDENING Kenneth Lemmon	15p
☐	76039 0	MOTHERCRAFT Ann Lynton	12½p
☐	76319 5	MONTH BY MONTH IN YOUR KITCHEN Daphne MacCarthy	12½p
☐	76052 8	LOOKING AFTER YOUR DOG Gordon Mack	12½p
☐	76043 9	THE DIET BOOK FOR DIET HATERS Derek Manley	15p
☐	76325 X	JAMS, CHUTNEYS AND PRESERVES Gladys Mann	15p

☐	76076 5	A PARENT'S GUIDE TO SEX EDUCATION Claire Rayner, S.R.N.	12½p
☐	76072 2	HOME NURSING AND FAMILY HEALTH Claire Rayner, S.R.N.	15p
☐	76046 3	HOUSEWORK—THE EASY WAY Claire Rayner, S.R.N.	12½p
☐	76058 7	DRESSMAKING—THE EASY WAY Marion Rotter	12½p
☐	76318 7	HANDWRITING Dorothy Sara	12½p
☐	76347 0	SHAPE UP TO BEAUTY Helen Speed	15p
☐	76053 6	THE THOUGHTFUL GIFT BUYER'S GUIDE Roma Thewes	12½p
☐	76322 5	NAME YOUR SON Roma Thewes	15p
☐	76323 3	NAME YOUR DAUGHTER Roma Thewes	15p
☐	76354 3	PATIENCE CARD GAMES FOR ALL THE FAMILY Wendy Riches and Roma Thewes	15p
☐	76361 6	COLLECTING SILVER AND PLATE Guy Williams	15p
☐	76357 8	COLLECTING VICTORIANA Guy Williams	15p
☐	76057 9	HOMEMADE WINE Rex Tremlett	15p
☐	76097 8	CREAM WITH EVERYTHING Lorna Walker	12½p
☐	76048 X	THE HOME-LOVER'S GUIDE TO ANTIQUES AND BRIC-A-BRAC Guy Williams	15p
☐	76049 8	DESIGN GUIDE TO HOME DECORATING Guy Williams	12½p
☐	76321 7	COLLECTING CHEAP CHINA AND GLASS Guy Williams	12½p
☐	76356 X	PALMISTRY (illustrated) Joyce Wilson	15p
☐	76316 0	DOWN LEFT WITH FEELING—THE UNPAID ACTOR'S HANDBOOK John Woodnutt	12½p
☐	76328 4	A CAREER FOR YOUR SON Henry Woolland	12½p
☐	76345 4	THE MAGIC OF HERBS Audrey Wynne-Hatfield	15p

All these books are available at your local bookshop or newsagent; or can be ordered direct from the publisher. Just tick the titles you want and fill in the form below.

CORGI BOOKS, Cash Sales Department, P.O. Box 11, Falmouth, Cornwall.
Please send cheque or postal order. No currency, and allow 4p per book to cover the cost of postage and packing in U.K., 6p per copy overseas.

NAME ....

ADDRESS ....

....